T0248075

Praise for *The Power of Culture*

"Thinking of starting a business? Read *The Power of Culture* first, carefully, and make sure it has a prominent place on your desk. Promoted to the corner office? Read *The Power of Culture* before you move in. Hunting for a job as you finish your MBA? Study *The Power of Culture* before you have your first interview. Laura Hamill knows what she's talking about, and she offers us a powerful guide to creating and sustaining humane and successful organisations. It's a great book!"

—Barry Schwartz, author of *Why We Work* and *The Paradox of Choice* and co-author of *Practical Wisdom*

"Culture can feel vague and amorphous, a silent force that impacts everyone but is owned by no one. *The Power of Culture* offers a comprehensive roadmap for understanding and harnessing the transformative potential of organisational culture. Blending real-world examples with insightful analysis, Hamill equips readers to proactively—rather than passively—shape culture. Essential reading for building aligned and values-driven workplaces."

—Elaine Lin Hering, author of *Unlearning Silence*

"With *The Power of Culture*, Laura Hamill delivers a thought-provoking exploration of how organisational culture impacts employee and organisational success. Grounded in both research and practical experience, Hamill provides actionable strategies for cultivating positive workplace cultures that prioritise humanity and purpose. This book is a must-read for anyone invested in creating environments where people flourish."

—Sir John Kirwan KNZM MBE, All Blacks rugby legend and co-founder and visionary of Groov

"The magic of this book is that it does something few books on corporate culture are able to do – which is make perhaps the most complex topic in the business world accessible to a very wide audience. No mean feat. Hamill brings clarity of thought and scintillating writing to the many facets, complexities and conundrums of culture, from the way it is thought of in academic circles to how it is operationalised in the C-Suite, to how it is made sense of by the average employee. In the process she brings us on a journey of discovery that completely illuminates this vast topic. In particular, her take on culture as how we experience it and her treatment of power in relation to culture are insightful and provocative. If you are able to read only one book on corporate culture, this is the one for you."

—David G. White, Jr, cognitive anthropologist and author of *Disrupting Corporate Culture*

The Power of Culture

The
Power of
Culture

Bringing Values to Life at Work

AN ECONOMIST EDGE BOOK

Laura Hamill

THE POWER OF CULTURE

Published with permission from *The Economist* by Pegasus Books.

The Economist is an imprint of
Pegasus Books, Ltd.
148 West 37th Street, 13th Floor
New York, NY 10018

First Pegasus Books cloth edition November 2024

ISBN: 978-1-63936-728-3

10 9 8 7 6 5 4 3 2 1

Printed in the United States of America
Distributed by Simon & Schuster
www.pegasusbooks.com

PEGASUS BOOKS
NEW YORK LONDON

For Keith, Griffin and Skylar

Contents

Introduction: Start with why

I grew up in the United States, in rural North Carolina. My parents were hippies – I mean real hippies – the VW van, tie-dyed T-shirts, back to nature, the whole thing. I even grew up in a log cabin that we built by hand. I didn't have electricity until I went to college. In a classic rebellion against my parents, I worked hard to be part of the "establishment" by getting straight As, earning a PhD and working in corporate America.

And I did well in "corporate". But perhaps unsurprisingly I learned that being part of the establishment wasn't all that I thought it was going to be. In fact, I learned that there was a lot that was broken about how organisations were run that helped me understand where my parents were coming from. My experiences with office politics, bad managerial and leadership behaviour, corporate policies with unintentional (but real) consequences, ineffective boards and struggles with balancing work I loved with raising children made me question my choices. Was this really what corporate life was about?

But then I started to have some amazing work experiences too. I began to see my work having a positive impact on other human beings. I was part of an organisation that had energy and positivity. And I started to believe that it was possible to have work that was meaningful and to work in organisations that not only function but also function well.

1

Why this book?

I'm a big believer in understanding why we do what we do. Clarity of purpose is important for everyone. I am grateful to have found a career that is meaningful to me and helps fulfill my sense of purpose. I thought it would be important for you, the reader, to understand why I wanted to write this book.

I'll start with the most obvious why. As an organisational psychologist, I have had the opportunity to work with many different organisations and have seen first-hand the impact that culture can have both on people and on the success of the business. I have seen the beauty of an aligned culture and the destructive atmosphere of toxic cultures. I have seen the impact on people and stock prices and have felt the pain of unhealthy cultures myself. Even for someone who has studied culture for decades, there is so much more still to understand. I believe that if more people know what organisational culture is about, we would be better placed to create positive cultures that underpin happier, more successful workplaces.

Second, over the course of my career, I have seen that culture is at the heart of many of the challenges that organisations face. I have worked for years on topics such as employee engagement, retention and well-being. I know that when you deeply understand each of these issues, you often conclude that there are cultural issues at their core.

That's because what's under the surface and deep down in all of us, as individuals and collectively, are the cultures we are part of: our national/geographical cultures, our professional cultures, our ethnic cultures and our organisational cultures (to name just a few). They have a large impact on what happens to us. It's imperative to understand what's really happening behind closed doors and underneath the surface. We all need to be thoughtful and intentional about the cultures we are a part of and that we all help to create.

Another reason I wanted to write this book is because I see the need to reconcile theoretical culture work with what really happens in organisations. There is a big gap between theory and practice here. In my career, I have been both the head of human resources and the leader of research studies on culture. In HR, there is real nitty-gritty, tactical and reactionary work. Every single day, you have no idea what kind of drama is going to come your way, and it's a hard job. It's difficult to have the time or energy to translate something as abstract and theoretical as culture into day-to-day work. At the same time, my work on the concept and theory of culture has shown me that the culture construct is a complex one; there's still a lot of disagreement among scholars about what it is and how to measure it.

Having both these perspectives has helped me understand many of the nuances that organisations face when trying to understand their cultures. I want to take the best of what we need to know about culture from an academic or conceptual perspective and combine that with what really goes down in organisations to make culture more accessible and more personal. I want to talk about culture not just at an organisational level, but also at a human level, with real examples of how culture impacts individual people.

Each of us can decide what role we want work to play in our lives. I've seen people successfully put work in a compartment and put it over *there*. And then say: "Okay, this culture is not really one that I personally connect with, but I still need this job. I still need a paycheque. But I can see it for what it is and maybe not be so miserable in it." But most people I know have difficulty with this kind of compartmentalisation. That's another reason I care about this so much. Maybe it's a call back to my roots of peace, love and happiness. Life is short. We shouldn't be miserable in our jobs.

Many books on culture are written for CEOs or heads of HR. But culture is not just relevant for those in leadership positions. Identifying culture, seeing it, talking about how it's impacting you and other people is for everyone at work. This book strives to democratise the understanding of culture by offering practical and relatable tools and approaches.

Now is a great time to be thinking about culture and work. The global pandemic forced us into thinking differently about where work has to happen (and how much we work) and what control and autonomy can look like in ways that we never have before. The many heart-breaking examples of social (especially racial) injustice have brought to the forefront the structures and systems that continue to oppress so many. And many are saying they are not interested in sacrificing everything for a paycheque; they are demanding that work becomes better than it is now.

Organisational culture is at the heart of these problems and at the root of their solutions.

What to expect in this book

I start by defining organisational culture and explaining why it is so difficult to understand. Every organisation has a culture, there's no question about that – any group of people that works together to achieve a goal will have a culture. But how do people experience the culture? I also discuss how important the experience of culture is and why it matters to organisations and to the people who work in them. Most organisations are unaware of how their culture is being experienced by employees and whether the culture is helping or hindering the organisation to achieve its goals.

Next, I introduce my core theme: how to be more intentional about culture and how to use the Intentional Culture Circle to operationalise the culture your organisation wants or needs (its aspirational culture). I walk readers through this approach and explain the steps that you can take to put the culture you need into place.

At the end of the book, I address some of the assumptions people tend to have about culture and why those assumptions need to be questioned. The book concludes with my aspirations for the kind of culture organisations should be focusing on – cultures that are more human-centric.

Culture has the power to create organisations where organisational and individual needs are aligned. It has the power to inspire and unite an entire workforce in the service of common goals. It can also help determine how leaders should lead and how managers should manage. It can be used to describe your company to potential partners, clients or employees, and provide an important comparison for any potential acquisitions or joint ventures. And it can ensure that the company is well positioned to meet its future business objectives, while creating meaning and purpose and a positive day-to-day experience.

Done well, culture can be a powerful and inspirational way for people and organisations to thrive. I hope this book helps you find more ways to do just that.

PART 1

Understanding culture

Overview

In the first part of this book, I cover the fundamentals of organisational culture: what it is, how it is related to climate and other similar ideas, and why it matters.

To start with, I define culture and describe how various characteristics of culture make it both interesting and elusive, especially when it comes to studying and evolving it. I discuss why company culture is so powerful in its ability both to shape individual behaviour and to create clarity, connection and inspiration for the people who work there.

In Chapter 2, the central theme revolves around the crucial relationship between the articulated and experienced culture within an organisation. This chapter highlights the importance of aligning aspirational culture with the actual experiences of employees, emphasising that culture is not just about what leaders articulate but also, more importantly, how employees experience it every day. The chapter stresses the need for organisations to actively manage the alignment between culture and various elements of their systems, practices and behaviours to ensure meaningful and aligned cultural experiences. The last part of the chapter looks at the evolving dynamics of workplace culture, particularly in the context of remote and hybrid working.

Chapter 3 delves into the broader implications of organisational culture on business and human outcomes. Various studies have demonstrated the positive relationship between a well-aligned culture and business success, but there are challenges in defining and measuring it. This chapter also explores the concept of toxic cultures and how culture can have a profound impact on people at work.

1

Defining culture

In the early 2000s, the Ford Motor Company was on the brink of bankruptcy. The company had lost about a quarter of its market and none of its brands was performing well. Stiff competition from Japan and high labour costs were also a cause for concern. Internally, there was a lack of unity, collaboration and trust. The culture was characterised by fear, especially fear of the leadership.

This was the turnaround challenge presented to the new CEO, Alan Mulally, when he took over in 2006.

An obvious area for change was financial planning and discipline, but Mulally brought a different perspective; he also focused on culture as a means of bringing the company together and boosting its performance.

He developed the One Ford approach, a set of behavioural expectations about how employees should work together across the company's entire global infrastructure. He encouraged leaders throughout the organisation to be transparent about the state of the business and speak honestly about what wasn't working. He held them accountable for the results they said they would achieve and for the behavioural expectations outlined in the One Ford approach. Bad leadership behaviour was unacceptable, and leaders who were not ready to adapt to the new standards were let go. The One Ford plan also outlined and reinforced global business models that could easily be replicated and executed around the world.

Ford has estimated that the change in strategy made overall product development two-thirds more efficient between 2006 and 2012. Making culture a core component of this turnaround – and making sure the new approach was taken seriously throughout the company – has been credited with saving Ford from bankruptcy and helping it to survive during the Great Recession of 2007–9.

Contrast this with the experience of Ernst & Young (EY) where, in 2022, employees were caught cheating on the ethics component of the exams they need to pass for their accounting jobs. The very auditors who work to ensure that other companies play by the rules were breaking the rules themselves, and there was evidence that this cheating had been going on for at least ten years.

A spokesperson for EY said: "At EY, nothing is more important than our integrity and our ethics. These core values are at the forefront of everything we do." And the values on their website seem to communicate just that: "People who demonstrate integrity, respect and teamwork. People with energy, enthusiasm, and the courage to lead. People who build relationships based on doing the right thing."

Interviews with the employees who were caught cheating said they knew that their cheating went against the company's core values, but they did it anyway, because they were struggling to pass the exams and because of heavy workloads.

Given the number of employees involved and that the cheating had been going on for a decade, there clearly was another, very different message being sent to employees at EY about what really mattered: not integrity or doing the right thing, but instead getting stuff done and passing exams so that they could get even more stuff done.

In addition to the $100m penalty that EY paid to the US Securities and Exchange Commission, EY will pay a very high price for the hit to its reputation, especially given the nature of its work.

The power of culture

These contrasting examples show the power of culture for organisations, their strategies and performance, their people and behaviours.

Get it right, and culture can be a positive force for good, improving performance as Mulally showed at Ford.

Get it wrong, as EY and companies as wide-ranging as Uber, Boeing, Volkswagen and the NFL have found, and culture can be a negative force, undermining performance and causing significant reputational damage.

A recent study from MIT/Sloan found that a toxic culture is by far the strongest predictor of employee attrition and is ten times more important than compensation in predicting turnover.[1] Employees themselves have never been as clear as they are now about the importance of their individual and collective experiences at work to their commitment to their employers.

In short, culture matters.

Any group of people that comes together to solve a problem or achieve a goal starts forming the ways that they collectively do things. Some of those ways are about the task at hand: how they break down the work, who does what, how fast they work. But other "ways we do things" are about how employees interact with the other people in their group.

- Do they interact frequently?
- Do they listen to each other?

- Do they take breaks? If so, do they still interact while they are pausing?
- Do they collaborate when they face challenges?
- Do they ask for input?
- How do managers and leaders interact with the rest of the team?

The questions can go on and on. There are accepted ways in which employees learn to behave with the group of people they work with, and these behaviours can become so accepted that people don't even realise that they are doing them.

But aren't these just typical human ways of interacting? Like making eye contact or smiling when greeting someone? Sure, many of those basic ways of interacting with humans are part of an organisation's culture. But there are other aspects of behaviour that can vary widely from organisation to organisation.

Take, for example, how employees interact with people in positions of power. In one organisation, employees who cross paths with a leader may say "Hi" and have a quick chat, whereas in another organisation that doesn't happen – employees look down when the leader walks by. As you can imagine, the ripple effects of these different styles of leadership interaction will make themselves felt in other ways, such as compliance, speaking up and taking risks.

What is culture?

Think back to how you felt when you started the job you are in now or your previous job. Do you remember how you felt on your first day? Your first week? Were there any culture "Ah-has" that clearly said to you: *This is how we do it here*? An organisation's culture is often crystal clear when you first join an organisation, but over time it becomes murky, almost unseeable.

Business theorist and psychologist Edgar Schein was one of the foremost experts on culture, and developed much of our understanding of what culture is and why it is so difficult to understand. For Schein, organisational culture is defined as:

> a pattern of shared tacit assumptions that was learned by a group as it solved its problems of external adaptation and internal regulation, that has worked well enough to be considered valid and, therefore, to be taught to new members as the correct way to perceive, think and feel in relation to those problems.[2]

In simpler terms, culture is the *collective set of reasons why employees behave the way they do within an organisation*. It is the backdrop for everything that happens there.

Think of the sum of what employees collectively believe about the organisation as a shared mindset. This mindset incorporates how people feel about the organisation and what they believe is valued, and it comes to life through behavioural norms. These norms are how people who are part of the organisation typically behave. How people think, feel and behave are all important aspects of understanding culture.

Sometimes this shared mindset is influenced by formal rules, like an employee handbook, policies or standards formally communicated by a manager. Employees also observe the existing systems and structures to learn about what is valued and what is not: for example, who are in leadership positions, how the organisation is structured, how performance is appraised. More often than not, though, the formation of the shared mindset is informal, unwritten and even unclear. Employees learn about it over time through a learning and adapting cycle.

This shared mindset becomes a set of guideposts for behaviour, defining what is accepted and what isn't. It becomes so ingrained and accepted that employees no longer even question it; it becomes automatic and unconscious. It's even been called an organisation's "silent language".[3] An analogy is thinking about culture like the water a fish swims in. Water is so fundamental to fish – so critical and core to their existence – that we can wonder whether they even have an awareness of it. That's how culture works too.

This shared mindset helps employees understand what is expected. Human beings seek predictability and understanding. They want the complex to be understood, and the cultural rules and norms that form this shared mindset help us make sense of this complexity.

It can be helpful to think about organisational culture as the "personality" of an organisation. An individual's personality can be described in words like being extravert or introvert, quiet or loud, involved or standoffish, for example. A person doesn't demonstrate these qualities all the time, but for the most part they do. They aren't one or the other (eg, involved or standoffish) but may be a little more or a little less of each. And personalities are multifaceted, too; you can't adequately describe someone's personality in just one word.

Organisations are similar. Multiple cultural descriptors can be true. They might not be consistently demonstrated by everyone, but they tend to be, and they aren't always one thing or another. This organisational "personality" helps us get to know the organisation, to understand what it is like. And before long, as employees adapt to it, they start to become part of it. What was once so easy to spot becomes a given, a shared mindset that is no longer in question.

The characteristics of culture

The very nature of culture is what makes it so interesting and so challenging. It's because of these characteristics that so many of us struggle to understand it. But by understanding these natural characteristics better, you can start to work "with" culture and not against it.

First, culture is **abstract**. It is difficult to pin down, difficult to describe and has multiple components.

Culture, by definition, is also **shared**. It exists only at the group level and more than one person is required for it to be experienced.

Culture is **dynamic** and **pervasive.** It flows through an organisation like a river, resulting in common behaviours, symbols, rituals, mindsets and approaches.

Culture is **relative**. For the most part, it's not accurate to say that culture is *absolutely* good or bad – culture is only *relatively* good or bad, according to how much it is helping your company achieve its goals.

Culture is **enduring.** It carries on consistently over time and is self-fulfilling because it attracts people who behave consistently with the culture and repels those who do not.[4]

Culture is **powerful** because it guides the behaviour of everyone in your organisation.

Finally and most importantly, culture is a fundamentally **human** idea. All culture work must involve the humans that are part of it. It is not about plans, processes or workflows (though these can be impacted by culture); it's about how human beings feel clarity, connection and inspiration.

For these reasons, culture often seems to be a mystery to most – a powerful and important one, but just out of reach for us to manage or understand.

So, let's dig into one way to understand culture better

– which is to break it down into understandable components, often called cultural attributes.

Cultural attributes

Just like components of an individual's personality, one mechanism for understanding an organisation's culture is to define its attributes. By breaking culture down into its component parts, you can start to understand each of them – and how each of these parts work together.

For example, the word pairs below describe potential elements in an organisation's culture. This list is not exhaustive, but it provides tangible examples to consider. You may find that one of the words in the list does a great job of describing your organisation. Or you may find that your organisation is somewhere in the middle, or leans towards one of the words but is not completely described by that word.

For example, you might feel that the culture is honest for the most part, but there are a couple of issues that tend to be kept as secrets – so you would probably think of this aspect of culture as leaning towards honest, but not completely on the right side of the continuum. Think of this list as a way to start thinking about the cultural attributes that describe your organisation.

Top-down decision-making	....	Participative decision-making
Rigid	....	Relaxed
Cold	....	Caring
Disjointed	....	Integrated
Focused on quantity	....	Focused on quality
Hierarchical	....	Flat
Micromanaged	....	Autonomous
Reactive	....	Proactive
Secretive	....	Honest
Relationship-saving	....	Truth-telling
Indifferent	....	Curious

It is important to understand the unique descriptors of your culture, and how they work together. For example, think about how being curious and caring might work differently with relationship-saving or with truth-telling. For an organisation that is curious, caring but also relationship-saving, there could be a tendency not to be honest when someone needs to hear difficult feedback. Over time, this can result in an organisation not addressing individual and organisational performance issues, which can have a serious impact on the ability of the organisation to meet its goals. Compare that with an organisation that is curious, caring and truth-telling. This combination of cultural attributes may be more likely to lead to individual and organisational success.

Cultural strength

As well as understanding the specific components of culture, the strength of the culture is also an important consideration. Organisational culture is often very pervasive and may be felt strongly across geographical and functional boundaries, from the top to the bottom. In some organisations, specific cultural attributes are strong and others are experienced more moderately or not at all. Cultural strength indicates how pervasively, consistently and clearly employees experience it.

In some organisations, especially large ones, there can be sub-cultures – that is, cultures within cultures – that employees feel a part of. These sub-cultures can detract from the overall strength of the overarching organisation's culture. Other times, these sub-cultures are beacons of light within a culture that is not thriving.

What cultural strength doesn't address is whether the overall culture or specific cultural attributes are helping or hindering the organisation's ability to achieve its strategy. You can have a strong culture, but it still might not be the culture the organisation needs and may even be holding the organisation back.

As you can see, the very nature of culture makes it challenging but also fascinating. You probably have an intuition about culture; you may fundamentally understand how much culture matters to your own experiences at work. This is another fascinating aspect of culture – understanding that culture matters to us, but not feeling like there are clear ways to impact it. In my mission to democratise culture, the first step is understanding what culture is; the next is being able to separate the actual culture from the culture the organisation needs or wants to have.

Actual culture vs the "aspire to" culture

Culture that is described for the purposes of recruiting or marketing (eg, what you find on company websites and in glossy brochures) is known as the "aspire to" culture.

The "aspire to" culture is the culture the organisation declares that it has or wants to have, or what the market/industry wants it to be or thinks it is; it's the culture we "aspire to". This "aspire to" culture is generally one that the organisation strives for, and it's often more employee friendly than the current culture. It typically supports a particular business need or a shift in business strategy.

In the early 2010s, there was an interesting phenomenon in tech companies – to see which companies could "out-fun" the others. From gigantic slides in the lobby to raucous parties to kickball teams, fun was a big focus. Some companies even included fun as one of their company values. Who can argue with having more joy in our lives? Not me. But for some companies there was an employee backlash for pushing mandatory fun. And many of these companies never connected the dots between why they wanted their employees to have fun and how this aligned to their "aspire to" culture.

Company **values** are often the way organisations articulate the "aspire to" culture. Sometimes, these values are created by the leadership team or an outside consultant. Other times, employees, managers and leaders work together to create them. Rarely, though, do organisations start with their business strategy when developing their values. Instead, they tend to create the values retrospectively without an explicit connection to what the company is trying to achieve.

Company values are often so non-descript that they could belong to any organisation. "Integrity" as a value is an example. Of course, there's nothing wrong with valuing integrity – in fact, it's a great thing. But many companies have included it in their values just to tick a box without clarifying how being honest and moral is important to their business and how that might show up on the ground. In other companies, especially start-ups, the values are so esoteric that it's hard for anyone outside the organisation to make sense of them.

It's important for someone outside an organisation (like a job candidate, a potential customer or investor) to be able to read the company's values and understand them. If they can see a connection between what they personally value and what the organisation values, they're more likely to want to work there. It's also important not to use insider language or acronyms or terms that only current employees can relate to.

Creating values, like creating the mission and vision of the company, is a fundamental step in declaring what the company is and what it stands for. Simply declaring the culture through the values doesn't make it real.

The "aspire to" culture can often be very different from the culture that people experience day to day. And if, as is often the case, there is a lack of understanding about what the current culture is, the gaps between the current culture and the "aspire to" culture are unknown.

A company I worked for rolled out its "aspire to" culture via email – not the most effective way to communicate something this important. The email came from the CEO with a subject line that made everyone open the email right away. As employees read the email, you could hear laughter down the hallway. They were reading the "aspire to" culture and laughing aloud about how ridiculous it was – it was so different from what they experienced every day. For example, the company was highly competitive internally and the email claimed it was collaborative. The key error was not acknowledging that the organisation wanted or *aspired* to move in that direction but that it was not there yet, and why it was important for the business to strive to get there at all.

Most organisational cultures are neither good nor bad. Rather, there tend to be aspects of the culture that are more positive or more negative, according to how well the culture supports the organisation to meet its goals and achieve its business strategy.

To be effective, culture needs to make sense or "align" to what the organisation is trying to achieve. It seems obvious that a company creating collaboration software should want to make sure that its employees are collaborating. And that if a company was trying to create brand new business opportunities that involve significant innovation and risk, it would need its employees to feel safe trying new things.

However, this explicit need for connection between what an organisation is trying to achieve and what its employees are experiencing is surprisingly rare. These aren't subtle nuances that need to be tweaked. These are large "in your face" disconnects.

And because of the importance of alignment with business strategy – and the wide variability in those strategies – there is no one size fits all for culture. Each organisation must determine which specific norms, values and beliefs will help it to succeed.

The disconnect between aspirational culture and business strategy

Why is it that organisations continue to have a disconnect between their "aspire to" culture and their business strategy? Here are some of the reasons.

- **The business strategy is unclear or not widely understood.** It's difficult to connect culture to a strategy that no one knows. Do people (and especially those working on culture) have a clear strategy to work with? Do they understand it?

- **Culture is being driven by people disconnected from the strategy.** Assuming that the business strategy is clear, are the employees (or consultants) working on culture privy to the strategy work? Have they had enough exposure to it to understand it?

- **Culture is thought of as an HR-only initiative.** In many organisations, focusing on culture becomes an HR responsibility. This happens when culture is thought of only in terms of people practices (like hiring and onboarding, or induction) instead of being core to overall company success.

- **Culture is a surface-level or "tick-box" initiative.** Some companies try to shortcut the culture work. They do this by thinking that if they just throw a couple of parties or put up some values on the wall, their work is done. But if the culture the company aspires to isn't relevant to where the company is and what people need, it might seem like something that the organisation is just going through the motions to create. If employees don't have an emotional connection to the culture and feel that it is relevant and important, the organisation isn't likely to get much traction.

- **It's hard work.** It's not easy to create this connection – it requires real thought and effort (and lots of input and iterations) to make the connections between business strategy and human emotion, cognition and behaviour explicit.

At Southwest Airlines, putting employees first is core to its culture. Its values are clearly articulated with a focus on behaviours like "Choose to do right", "Don't take yourself too seriously" and "Embrace team over self". I once had the opportunity to attend one of its regional all-hands meetings. The messages I heard from the leaders and presenters during this meeting were consistent with these "aspire to" values. The emphasis on topics that mattered to employees was clear. One of the biggest things I noticed was that employees were seriously engaged in that meeting. Even though we were in a large stadium and people were relatively anonymous, no one was secretly checking their phone. They stayed the whole time, and they were leaning forward in their seats listening to every word. They wanted to be there. The behaviour of both leaders and employees during that meeting brought their values to life.

Southwest employees also demonstrate a consistency between how they treat each other and how they treat their passengers, even when they have faced some significant bumps in the road. The airline has experienced technical issues because of out-of-date technology, with some even claiming that the organisation is riding on the back of its people-first culture and not addressing fundamental operational issues.

But it still gets results. Southwest Airlines continues to receive awards for being a great place to work and for being an outstanding economy airline.[5]

Culture guides our behaviour

When people first start working in an organisation, they begin to discover how things work. From explicit onboarding and training to subtle eye movements and facial gestures, they uncover what is considered acceptable and whether they want to change their behaviour to conform to those expectations (or not). During every hour of the day, employees are guided by culture. Should they collaborate or compete? Should managers react quickly or create longer-term structure and plans? Should people participate in company discussions or stay quiet?

This new employee culture socialisation begins with an anticipation of what the organisation's culture is going to be, before the employee even starts work there. This anticipation is built on perception: from social media, brand perceptions, friends and acquaintances, and from the few pre-hire interactions they may have had with recruiters and hiring managers. This understanding becomes deeper during their experience with their first days of work and onboarding. Within the first days, weeks and months an employee's cultural understanding becomes more and more formed. They start to understand what they are supposed to do and how they are supposed to behave. The "way things are done around here" starts to form.

The cultural web model, developed by Gerry Johnson,

Richard Whittington and Kevan Scholes, is a framework used to understand how we come to develop our understanding of culture.[6] It identifies the interconnected elements that shape the culture of an organisation.

- People start to understand culture through the **rituals and routines** that represent the daily activities and behaviours within an organisation.
- **Symbols** (also called artifacts) encompass the visible representations of the organisation, such as logos and titles, which convey meaning and identity.
- **Stories** are the narratives shared between employees, conveying history, values and lessons, shaping the organisation's identity.
- **Organisational structure** represents the formal hierarchy, roles and reporting lines, illustrating power distribution within the organisation.
- **Control systems** – policies, procedures and measures – guide people's behaviour and performance.
- **Power structures** indicate the formal and informal power relationships within the organisation, reflecting who holds influence and decision-making authority.

This model emphasises the interconnectedness of these elements, suggesting that altering one element can impact the entire organisational culture. It also shows that messages about what is valued come to the employee from many different directions. When culture is learned in this way, cultural messages are typically not clear and direct statements of what the culture is about. Instead, there are "bits of meaning" that employees take in and accumulate.[7] These bits accumulate into a "cultural toolkit" that becomes more and more robust over time.

Employees draw on these tools in their cultural toolkit to decide how to react to a given situation. Because of this, one employee might respond in a different way to another employee in the same situation. They might have built a different cultural toolkit, or they might not have as many cultural tools to draw from. So, individuals have some choice and agency in how they interact with their organisation's cultures; they are not culture victims. Although their behaviour is influenced greatly by the culture, they can still choose how they are going to respond. This choice, however, is influenced by many factors, including past experiences, and formed beliefs about their own power and the power of others.

In my first week at one company, I was asked to write a memo that would be distributed widely in the organisation. Because my manager didn't seem very accessible, I asked my team member next door to give me feedback on it. After giving her a day to review, I knocked on her door and asked if she had had a chance to read it. She looked at me and said: "It's fine."

As I walked back to my office, I realised there wasn't any feedback on the document, and no indication that she had read it at all. So what did I learn? I learned that in this company (from this interaction and others), we don't ask other people for feedback and, even more harshly, I realised I was on my own. This message was reinforced by my manager during my first performance review a few months in. He told me to stop helping other people and to focus more on tooting my own horn.

I'd like to say I took the high road and rejected this advice. But I didn't. I learned what was valued and started to fit in culturally. In retrospect, I really wanted to be part of that organisation and identified with it. I did not feel I had the power to make a different choice. Before long, I realised I was behaving in ways that were similar to what I had experienced when I started: I was now part of the culture. In fact, I was such a part of it, I was no longer aware of my own behaviour.

Those who catch on and conform are more likely to stay in the organisation, whereas those who don't catch on and don't adapt to these new ways of doing things will likely leave – either by their own choice or by that of the organisation. Sometimes organisations label these people who are not able to adapt as "bad hires" instead of understanding that it may instead be a lack of cultural adaptation.

Cultural adaptation is a cycle of observing, learning and integrating. As Johnson, Whittington and Scholes showed, the inputs to this cycle are everywhere in the organisation, from physical artifacts like how the office is decorated, to the organisational structure, to the behaviours observed in others.

There are many ways in which employees learn culture, including:

- intentional learning (eg, onboarding)
- role models
- team member interactions
- stories
- rituals, routines and traditions
- symbols and artifacts
- structures
- systems
- what gets rewarded
- what is prioritised
- who gets promoted
- who has power
- who is hired, who is fired.

Much of this adaptation happens when employees are new to an organisation, but they continue to learn the nuances of the culture throughout their employment.

This is why culture is so powerful: it shapes people's behaviour, guides their decisions and helps them determine what to do next. And because culture is at the root of all behaviour in an organisation, if it isn't healthy or aligned to strategy, it can have very negative consequences. But on the flip side, culture can help create extremely positive climates, engaged and productive employees, and outstanding business results.

Fundamentally, culture is a means for the organisation to create clarity, connection and inspiration which leads to better outcomes for employees and for the organisation.

Culture as clarity allows employees and the organisation to be more focused on what matters and to be clear about what the expectations are for how they behave and interact with others. It sets a standard for what each employee can expect from others, including managers and leaders.

Culture as connection helps to fulfill a fundamental need that humans have to connect with other human beings through meaningful interactions and relationships. This connection helps reduce feelings of isolation and loneliness, and can increase feelings of inclusion and belonging.

Culture as inspiration acknowledges that there is something bigger that has meaning and purpose that employees are all doing together. They are part of something that is making a difference in the world.

What culture is NOT

Anything that is related to how employees feel about their work can often be put into the culture bucket. This is one more reason why culture continues not to be understood and not to be improved in most organisations.

It is important to be clear and precise about what culture is and what it is NOT.

- **NOT benefits, perks or compensation.** Although those send clear messages about what is valued and what is not valued in the organisation, by themselves (without the accompanying understanding of what is being reinforced), they are not culture.

- **NOT the climate.** Climate and culture go hand in hand, but how an organisation feels is different to WHY it feels that way. For example, a company you work at might feel really busy. Busy is how you would describe the climate. WHY it feels busy would be the culture. And figuring out the why takes some digging. Is it because of recent errors that may indicate a lack of focus on quality? Or because of an intense focus on innovation? Or perhaps an impending visit from a leader who people don't trust? There could be many cultural explanations. Again and again, organisations confuse climate and culture – which I'll explore in more detail in Chapter 2.

- **NOT about the individual.** By definition, culture happens only at the group level. It is about our shared values, norms and beliefs and requires other human beings to even exist. It is typically measured and acted on at the organisational level, rather than at the team or individual level.

- **NOT an oversimplified singular focus.** Human beings have a desire to simplify; we love to break down complex ideas into a simple label or colour or acronym. In the early days of studying organisational culture, that's what the researchers did too. They studied culture types with the idea of summarising this complex construct with one word like "authoritarian" or "adhocracy". The research, however, does not support this overly simplistic approach.[8] Instead, it's important to be more holistic and thorough, thinking about culture as a set of attributes that work together in unique ways given the organisational context. This is why it is important for organisations to stop using terms like "culture of learning" or "culture of well-being" or "culture of performance". These ideas are only one part of a more complex system. And it's especially important for each department not to push its own "culture of X", which can happen, especially in large organisations. Focusing on "culture of X" feels like a fad to employees and can be confusing when the "culture of Y" comes along.

- **NOT Margarita Fridays, massage chairs or ping pong tables.** Occasionally, I'll search jobs that have culture in their title. More often than not, they are basically event planner jobs. Parties and employee get-togethers can be fun and have a positive impact on your employees. But if they are not accompanied by the hard culture work (like that described in this book), they will not have the impact you were hoping for.

- **NOT new office space**. When referring to the conditions of their work, employees, managers and leaders often think about their physical surroundings and don't think about the deeper culture. Office space can be a temporary injection of "new and shiny" into the daily routine but will never be a substitute for the impact that culture has on how people feel about their work.

- **NOT leadership propaganda.** Culture should not be a mandate from above. Done right, culture is a source of connection and inspiration – and everyone must feel a part of it for it to land.

We are part of many cultures

Of course, our work culture isn't the only culture that influences us. Many of us are part of other groups of people – clubs, sports teams, schools, religious groups, families. These groups also have their own sets of values, norms and beliefs. Professions can also have cultures – think of the potential norms, values and beliefs for people who are attorneys, teachers, construction workers or nurses.

Another important influence is the culture of the country or region of the world you live in. How things are done in a particular part of the world will influence the culture of an organisation that is part of that country or region. Sometimes it is hard to decide whether a particular aspect of an organisation's culture is professional, national/geographical or organisational.

Work isn't a new construct. Human beings have been working together towards shared goals for a long time. So why are we still trying to understand culture? And why do organisations keep trying to do surface-level things to impact it?

The complexity of culture is one reason for the continued struggle to create aligned cultures. Culture *is* a complex construct and one that even academics are still learning.

And when we aren't aware of how the culture is affecting our behaviour, it's difficult to realise the impact it is having. Our understanding of culture and power, and how they both influence behaviour, continues to evolve.

But it is possible for organisations to navigate what might seem like a minefield. Companies like Ford and Southwest

Airlines have demonstrated that they can create the clarity, connection and inspiration that employees desire and businesses need. But there's still significant culture work that most organisations need to undertake. Despite the complexity and ambiguity, organisations must work on being intentional about their cultures: people's experience and the success of their businesses depend on it.

Remember

1. Culture is a multifaceted, complex and often misunderstood set of attributes that need to be aligned to business goals.

2. Culture is important to understand because it guides employees in how to behave in organisations. Without this cultural alignment it is difficult for organisations to achieve their goals.

3. Culture is a means for the organisation to create clarity, connection and inspiration which leads to better outcomes for employees and for the organisation – and yet most organisations fail to be intentional about culture and continue to struggle.

In the next chapter, I dig into what it means for employees to experience organisational culture. Without creating intentional, experienced cultures, cultural efforts will fall flat. Whatever a company might say on its website, it's what *really* happens every day, and how those experiences impact human lives, that matters.

2

Culture as an experience

Amy rode the lift to the top floor of the building, excited to meet the leadership team of the company that she had just joined. The lift doors opened, and she could see lots of people already sitting at the large conference room table behind the glass wall. What was odd, though, was that everyone was sitting quite still. The feeling was very formal and serious, and when she entered the room there were two people at the head of the table, whispering to each other while everyone else stayed silent.

After a few awkward minutes, the CEO (one of the two at the end of the table) started the meeting, which was primarily a meet and greet, with Amy sharing her background and her plans for her new role at the company. Before arriving, Amy had been excited about this opportunity to meet the leadership team, and she wasn't that nervous. But once she got into the room, that changed.

Her sense of humour and the rapport that she usually had when she gave presentations were met with none of the usual smiles and nods of encouragement. Instead, the leadership team members seemed uncomfortable, even unhappy. It was hard for Amy not to take this personally.

Despite the awkwardness, Amy made it through her presentation. But she left the meeting feeling awful. Now she wondered if there was something she had done wrong in her presentation. And she also wondered if she had made the wrong choice in taking this job.

What Amy experienced when those lift doors opened and during that meeting was climate: how an organisation "feels". Later, Amy would learn that her first experience gave her some signs about the culture, but it would take a while to find out why the meeting participants were acting the way they did. Over time, Amy would come to understand that the culture of this organisation was unhealthy and misaligned and was hindering the company's ability to achieve its ambitious strategy.

Culture matters only if, and how, it is experienced. The best cultural intentions mean nothing; what matters is how people experience it on the ground.

Think of culture as the roots of the organisational tree. You know the roots hold the tree upright and provide nutrients and water to the rest of the tree. But you don't see the roots. What you see are the trunk, the branches, the leaves.

Culture comes to life throughout the rest of the "tree" of the organisation. The alignment between the culture, the strategy and purpose, the climate, and the policies and practices all work together to create the tree that people can see and feel.

An organisation is also impacted by the world around it, just like a physical tree is affected by the quality of the soil, sunshine and water. The industry, economic conditions, political climate, regulations and many more factors impact the entire organisation, including the culture.

Culture is a great example of a system. Many factors impact culture, which in turn influences other factors and outcomes. That's why culture can feel so dynamic and so hard to put your finger on.

Articulated vs experienced culture

More organisations are starting to tackle culture. Unfortunately, many are focusing on culture at a superficial level and not ensuring that culture is demonstrated and experienced consistently by all employees.

When an "aspire to" culture differs significantly from the reality that people experience day to day, leaders and organisations lose credibility. People are acutely aware when leaders aren't walking the talk. So there's an obvious disconnect when employees aren't experiencing what leaders have articulated.

But there are also other ways in which the articulated culture and the experienced culture can either be at odds or be aligned (see Figure 1).

When a company has done little or no work on its culture, there is a **cultural void**. Its "aspire to" culture has not been articulated and people have no consistent or intentional experience of it. And where there is a cultural void, other norms, values and beliefs will be created as employees seek to make sense of their complex world.

When a company has a cultural void, there is an overall feeling of mediocrity and the lack of anything special about the organisation, because there is no intention and no explicit experience of the culture. Remember: any group of people who work together to achieve a shared goal will have a culture. So there will be a culture, but in this situation, the culture isn't likely to help move the company or its people forward.

In other situations, there's a **leadership gap**, when people show that they are experiencing the culture but it hasn't been articulated clearly by the organisation. This represents a missed opportunity for leaders to connect culture with business strategy and to inspire people in the work that they are doing.

Figure 1: **Articulated and experienced culture**

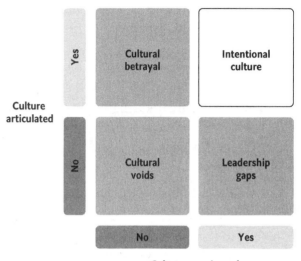

Culture
articulated

Culture experienced

In this situation, the culture is coming to life despite the leaders. It can happen when there has been a leadership transition or a series of acquisitions, and the new leaders have not been proactive about the culture they hope to create. The existing culture will linger. This can also happen when a strong HR function has put in place culturally aligned practices, but when the rest of the business leadership team is not driving culture home.

When the culture is articulated by the organisation but the experienced culture is different from what's been articulated, there is a sense of **cultural betrayal**. Employees can feel resentful that what they were "sold" about the organisation is not what they received. This can have a significant impact on emotional well-being, especially in mission-driven companies. The impact of this betrayal can run deep, leading to negative feelings about the company, withdrawal behaviours (like not participating in company meetings and events) and attrition.

But when the "aspire to" culture is articulated and is consistent with what employees are experiencing, **intentional culture** is alive and well.

How employees experience culture is perhaps even more important than whether an organisation has articulated the culture it wants to have. Unfortunately, many organisations tend to stop the culture work after they have posted their values on their website, not realising that they are only at the beginning of the journey.

Culture and climate

When employees use words like "fun", "busy" or "friendly", they are describing the climate – what it feels like to work in the organisation. When you dig deeper into finding out why the organisation is fun, busy or friendly (or, in Amy's example at the start of this chapter, silent, formal and whispering), you will uncover the organisational culture.

Climate is the set of more observable aspects of working in the organisation and can be felt right away. Culture is the set of rules that an employee comes to learn over time, often learning the norms of the organisation by trial and error, and seeing which behaviours are expected and rewarded.

In my example, Amy had some initial feelings about the organisation (which described the climate). After leaving that conference room and starting her job, she began to see why the meeting participants from her first day were acting as they were.

The CEO and COO were unpredictable and intimidating, making blistering statements like: "Is that the best you can do?" or "There's no way this is going to work." Projects and budgets were often cut without any input from those working on them and although there were innovative strategic initiatives, new projects were developed with outside consultants being given the most exciting work. Some leaders went along with this way of interacting and a few didn't (they spoke up when they felt the organisation was headed in the wrong direction). Those who didn't go along with what the CEO and COO did and said were continuously berated and eventually forced out of the organisation. Employees soon learned that it was better to keep their heads down and just do their jobs.

The CEO and COO were always together and were continuously whispering to each other during meetings and in the halls, with rumours swirling that they were having an affair. They were creating a culture characterised by fear, unfairness and impropriety. Amy's initial experience of the climate during her first day slowly led to her having a deeper understanding of the culture.

Climate and culture are inextricably connected – culture drives climate and climate impacts culture. Any changes in one must consider the other. If you are trying to change some aspect of the climate, you must understand and incorporate culture. If you are trying to change culture, you must incorporate aspects of the climate. For example, it is near impossible to create a requirement that employees collaborate more if the culture is clearly individualistic. However, if a new performance review system is put into place that rewards collaboration, this aspect of the climate will, over time, help to shift the culture.

Because every company's culture is different, it is difficult to generalise about culture from one company to another. That's why so much of the early research on culture was based on case studies rather than large-scale quantitative research studies. Think of climate as the **action of culture** and that culture can

Figure 2: **Examples of systems, practices and behaviours**

System examples	Practice examples	Behaviour examples
• People system • Management system • Leadership system • Employee listening system • Learning system • Organisational structure • Revenue system • Value creation and innovation • Financial system • Planning and strategy system	• Hiring • Onboarding • Performance management • Compensation • Succession planning • Learning and development • Termination • Employee surveys • Company meetings and town halls • Quarterly business reviews • Planning sessions	• Leader behaviour • Manager behaviour • Employee behaviour • Team member/peer behaviour • Direct reports' behaviour

help you understand why all those things matter and why they happen as they do. The practices are where you can observe and experience the culture.[1]

Culture is about the collective norms, values and beliefs of the organisation – the shared mindset that influences why we do what we do. **Climate** is about the experience (or action) of culture and is manifested through three primary mechanisms (see Figure 2).

- **Systems**: a set of integrated practices that work together to solve an overarching problem
- **Practices**: specific and discrete aspects of a system
- **Behaviour**: how people who are part of the system act.

The experience of culture breaks down when there is a lack of alignment between culture and an organisation's systems, practices and behaviour. For real change to occur, it must be confronted on multiple fronts (see Figure 3).

The systems, practices and behaviours of climate can reinforce culture by deciding who is selected into the organisation, who receives the most rewards and recognition,

Figure 3: **Climate and culture are connected**

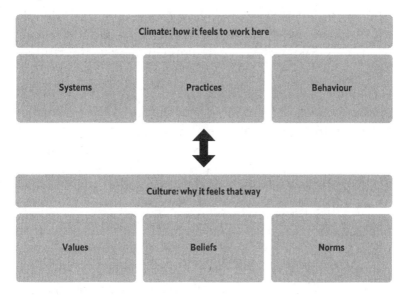

and who is promoted. New systems and practices that are not in line with the culture are likely to be rejected.

Take, for example, a medium-sized company acting on the results of an employee engagement survey. Those results indicated that people wanted more flexible options for working from home. The HR team put together a compelling flexible work programme including training managers, creating a set of criteria for taking part in the programme and rolling out a tool to help employees sign up. But six months later, only a few employees had done so.

Why was this the case? The HR team soon found out that the CEO had been walking the halls (known to employees as the 5pm walk), checking to see who was still at their desks. People had learned that what was really valued by the CEO was being seen in the office. Taking advantage of the new flexible work policy was not in line with that expectation.

Culture sends the clear message of what really matters to those in positions of power. Of course, the HR team had assumed (and hoped) that they were aligned with the culture when they designed this new programme, but the cultural message being sent by the CEO was stronger.

In this example, the HR team had used a measurement system (the engagement survey) to make a change to a practice (the work-from-home options). But because of the values and beliefs exhibited by the CEO (walking the halls and looking for who was at their desks), the behaviour and norms of working from home were rejected.

It's a high bar to have tight alignment between the culture and the systems, practices and behaviours that make up an organisation's climate. And even the most culturally aware company isn't likely to get it right all the time. But this alignment is almost impossible if you don't start with a strong clarity about the culture you intend to have.

You must build the cultural foundation first.

Engagement

Employee engagement is an idea most organisations have embraced and that's a good thing. The more emotionally connected people feel to their work, the more likely they are to do their best work. When that happens, the more likely an organisation is to achieve its goals.

However, organisations have tended to only focus on engagement in terms of their people – that is, hiring people who have the propensity to be engaged and reinforcing them to continue to be engaged. Unfortunately, our overemphasis on people being hyper-engaged for long periods of time is one of the contributing factors to employee burnout.

Instead, organisations need to understand and emphasise

the conditions they can create to support employees to be engaged: climate and culture.

Most employee engagement surveys try to measure these conditions from a climate perspective: for example, the availability of learning opportunities, clear goals or one-to-ones with a manager.

But most employee engagement surveys fail to ask about the cultural conditions that support engagement. Is there support for employee learning and growth in the organisation? Do employees feel empowered to make decisions? Is power shared throughout the organisation? Is there openness and honesty at every level? Do managers and leaders genuinely care about the well-being of employees?

Culture is almost always missing from these important (and well-established) measurement systems.

Employees are active participants in culture

It's important to remember that employees are not passive recipients of the culture and climate. They use what they understand about the culture to inform the decisions they make and how they behave. They also have the choice not to blindly accept the culture and climate.

Culture and climate may create more of a connection with certain employees in certain situations. For example, sociologist Ann Swidler believes that it's more likely that people will accept a new culture when they themselves feel settled.[2] When people feel unsettled, they are more likely to push back on the culture and climate.

Employees are also more likely to buy in to an organisation's purpose and goals when they believe that the culture is authentic and aligned with what they personally value (see Chapter 9 for more on personal values).

The physical workplace and culture

The physical workplace has long been one relatively easy (or at least tangible) way for leaders to demonstrate the aspirational culture. For example, if leaders want collaboration to be the norm, the workplace could physically manifest that with shared workspaces and common areas. Without a space where employees can regularly come together, there are fewer human-to-human interactions. And fewer in-person interactions with managers, leaders and colleagues mean fewer opportunities to learn about the culture through other people. Unsurprisingly then, the physical workplace has played a prominent role in culture formation.

Since the covid-19 pandemic, this relatively easy opportunity has changed with so many employees working from home. Many are fine with that tradeoff. More flexibility, no commute? Sign us up! But coming together face to face every day in physical places sends clear messages about what really matters. And not doing that comes with negatives. Organisations face real challenges in bringing their culture to life in tangible ways now that they can no longer depend on physical spaces to help them.

When new employees undergo a socialisation process, they look to many different inputs to start learning what the culture is about. The physical surroundings can send a message about things like the history of the organisation, how personal and warm it feels, how formal or informal it is, whether being similar or being different is valued, and whether employees have the autonomy to personalise their spaces. These physical manifestations of the culture give us the office vibe – whether it feels positive and energetic or dull, drab and depressing.

In the United States, there was a rapid rise in remote and hybrid work from 8.2% to 35.2% between February and May

44

2020.[3] And it seems that this will not revert to pre-pandemic levels, with many organisations shifting to completely remote workforces or post-pandemic remote work policies. One study found that 71% of hiring managers indicated that they were planning to keep or increase remote work in their organisations.[4]

It's easy to see the advantages for employees with this increase in remote and hybrid work. Research indicates that remote and hybrid employees reported less stress and being more productive than those who were in an office environment, as well as better physical and mental health.[5,6]

But it's important to acknowledge that the many jobs that require employees to be at work in person will continue to have the culture signals from the physical workplace. And many companies are in the tough position of trying to build and reinforce culture with some employees who work from home and others who are in the office, store or clinic.

Not enough time has yet passed to assess the impact that remote and hybrid working has on culture. But initial indications are that there are some important cultural implications from this shift.

Many remote and hybrid employees report **working more** than when they were in the office (55% say they work more hours working remotely).[7] And for many, with no clear start and end to the day (like your evening commute), the lines between work and home are blurred, making it easier to feel like you are working around the clock.

Employees also report that they feel **more isolated and lonely** working from home (71% say they are more distant from their coworkers; 54% say they have drifted apart from their colleagues).[8] And employees experience fewer informal interactions with colleagues when they are working from home; they don't just run into each other in the hallway. People who work from home also interact and collaborate less often with employees they don't know as well, compared with employees who work in the office. A study by Microsoft found that employees who work from home stayed in their silos more than those in the office.[9]

Interactions with managers are also more formal when working from home compared with working in the office. Because of the lack of visibility about what their employees are working on and reduced feelings of control, **manager power is threatened**. Managers can see whether employees in the office are working hard; they can stop by and ask for help or input. In theory, employee work outcomes and results could and should speak for themselves. But many jobs don't have widgets that you can count at the end of each day to determine productivity.

This power threat can impact the employee and manager relationship with managers exhibiting more controlling behaviours, like monitoring and asking for proof of work, plus reduced feelings of psychological safety (the belief that you won't be punished for speaking up or making mistakes) and trust for employees. **This feeling of power threat extends up the management chain.** And this is probably one of the reasons why some leaders are demanding that their employees come back to the office.

Some organisations also seem to be experiencing a **lack of employee participation** in company events (virtual and in-person), perhaps due to the overwork and blurred lines between work and home. These company events are often how the connection and sense of belonging and commitment are created and reinforced.

So what's the solution? How do you evolve how you form

and transform culture without the physical workplace and fewer in-person interactions?

It's clear that some things probably won't work, like forcing people to come into the office to interact and or to participate in surface-level fun activities over video calls. Forced fun never works. Perhaps we will look back on this time and think about our dreary offices coupled with long commutes as an old school way of embedding culture. But what will replace it? Who knows for sure, but new technology platforms, more meaningful employee interactions, and rethinking the roles of manager and leader are likely to be part of the solution.

Using new tools to interact

Obviously, one of the biggest technology changes with more remote work is using video-based remote meeting software like Zoom and MS Teams. But there are other tools that help with project coordination, document sharing and communication. Some seem only to replicate what in-office interactions looked like. But other tools seem to offer different ways of interacting with colleagues, creating new norms and new ways of forming culture.

Tim, a leadership and development employee at a technology company, works completely from home. He is a strong advocate for the use of the collaboration tool Slack.[10] He believes that the features of Slack allow for culture formation and reinforcement at the global tech company he works for. Tim thinks that because there are so many different channels for chatting, interacting and sharing, employees feel they are more deeply connected to each other, that they are part of something bigger and they really belong.

In Tim's words: "I think of the proverbial office culture as typified by the water cooler and stopping over at the desk ...

it becomes the social connections that you build based on common interest. It becomes the jargon that you use, the acronyms. And I think with Slack, they design it in such a way as to enable all those things to be emulated."

The way Tim and his colleagues interact using this technology platform helps them feel that different aspects of themselves are valued. Maybe it's about gardening, or about your dog, or being a parent or maybe it's about a specific project or work location. All these different identities are recognised through different channels and allow the employees in this global organisation to feel connected with each other.

It's also been argued that tools like Slack create a more equal playing field for people who are multilingual or who are more introverted, offering them more of an equal voice – valuing all, not just the "loud sales bro who's just talking about the game over the weekend, who dominates the conversation".

I gained another interesting perspective on this topic from the founder of Kumospace, Brett Martin. Kumospace is virtual office software that offers an online place for employees to work together. In my talk with him, we met in that virtual space, and I was surprised at how easy it was to navigate. Many of the typical ways we build culture in physical spaces are part of this software – like overall office vibe with colours and themes, pictures on the walls, customised desk decor, common spaces and company awards on the shelf. Brett's point is that we don't need to be binary about being in the office or being at home for our work. There can be another option, which is virtual.

Technology, like Slack and Kumospace, is likely to play a significant role in how culture formation and transformation happen in the future. Organisations should work to understand how technology could help fill in the gaps in their cultures depending on where, when and how employees are working.

Creating more meaningful connections

One of the errors many of us have made when moving to more remote work is to assume that you need to have more virtual interactions. But it's not about having more small talk or more superficial interactions. (No more virtual happy hours or trivia nights, please.) It is about creating higher quality virtual interactions and thoughtfully designed in-person interactions. Carefully designed and curated interactions help to create more meaning for employees.

For culture formation, the employee onboarding experience is critical. This is one of the best opportunities to interact with employees when they are the most open to listening. Onboarding done right should have a large focus on the aspirational culture, and it should be more curated and meaningful than one slide in an onboarding deck that lists the values. It should include other employees talking about the culture in person or in a video, a summary of the behavioural expectations that align to the values, a connection to the purpose of the company, and how important it is that each employee understands all these things.

I continue to hear stories about people coming into an empty office only to participate in Zoom calls. There should be a reason (other than because someone said so) for employees to come together and that needs to be connected to the business strategy. Organisations can be thoughtful about the kind of work that makes the most sense to do at home (work that is individual and task-focused) versus the kind of work that makes the most sense to do in the office (work that requires brainstorming and collaboration).

On top of that, organisations should make the time for culture work, both in person and virtually, using in-person time for people to get to know each other as people, rather than just as colleagues. Another related idea is to have employees design and determine when and how they want to get together. They are best placed to know which aspects of their work could use some input from their team members.

Rethink the roles of managers and leaders

The roles of managers and leaders are, of necessity, changing. Instead of feeling that their power is threatened and doubling down on control when team members work from home, managers and leaders should work to address the loneliness and isolation their colleagues are feeling. They can do this by creating more connection with their team – starting with understanding them as human beings. And with this understanding, managers and leaders should be offering people enriching work, better information, more development opportunities and more purpose.

Managers and leaders also need to be clearer about expectations. This lack of clarity about what success looks like is a weak spot for most organisations. With fewer in-person interactions that allow for feedback and course correction, this clarity is critical.

One biotech company I worked with required some employees to come into the office (because they are part of the manufacturing division of the company), while others in the organisation (like the scientists who created the new drugs) worked primarily from home. There was a growing resentment between the manufacturing division and the scientists, with those in manufacturing generally feeling resentful about their commutes and perceived lack of autonomy and freedom. Another source of resentment was that it seemed that those who were not in the office were not readily available or responsive.

The first reaction from the CEO was to demand that everyone

come into the office 100% of the time, because some employees had to be present. However, the ability to work from home had become a significant part of why the scientists (who also were highly skilled, highly marketable and difficult to replace) liked their work. So, after further thought and discussion, the leadership team decided to set clearer expectations for how the two groups should work together, centred around their values. First was being clear that they needed the whole company to work together as one team and that all roles supported the drugs they were developing and the lives they were saving. This made clear the important relationship between the scientists and manufacturing and that both teams were critical to the success of the business.

The CEO also clarified expectations around supporting the well-being of all employees – that the work was hard, but also that he cared about the employees as human beings and that they all should have flexibility and autonomy in what they do, sharing specific ways in which those in the manufacturing division would be offered more flexibility. There was also a clear expectation about the responsiveness of those working from home to those in the office and that they should support each other. They also educated and empowered leaders and managers to make sure that employees understood and embodied these expectations, course correcting where necessary.

These new expectations created more clarity and more connection between employees. It reminded and inspired employees about the important work they were doing. Being intentional about cultural expectations will go a long way to create the clarity needed to bring your culture to life.

Remember

1. Culture only matters if and how it is experienced.

2. Climate and culture are closely connected. Organisational systems, practices and behaviour must all be aligned with culture.

3. The physical workplace is a relatively easy way to embed culture; without it, organisations must develop new models for demonstrating culture.

4. Using new tools to interact, creating more meaningful connections, and rethinking the roles of managers and leaders are some of the ways to focus on culture with remote work.

Now that I have set the stage about what culture is and how important the experience of culture is, the next chapter provides evidence for how important culture is to organisations and to the humans who work in them.

3

Why culture matters

Typically, when it comes to company culture, people tend to think about big company names like Netflix or Microsoft. But the following story is an example of how culture impacts real people.

Jennifer lives in Nevada, in the United States. When she started work at a new job at a tech company, she immediately invested everything she had into her role. Before long, her work ethic led to her promotion, where she oversaw two teams.

Jennifer describes the company as small and family-like. Her performance reviews (and compensation) over her three and a half years of employment there reflected the company's appreciation of her hard work. Jennifer felt like an integral part of the company and was excited about her future there.

But there were some real challenges. In her opinion, the company was mostly concerned about turning a profit. Little emphasis was placed on valuing employee input or experience. And although the company offered unlimited time off, paid parental leave and some other perks, the culture was, for the most part, "all lip service" when it came to respecting what employees had to share about the company's practices or valuing them as people.

And this was reflected in Jennifer's workload. The stress was high and she was often sacrificing time with her family, working more than 16 hours a day. She was tired all the time, and felt she was always giving more and more.

Jennifer felt that what was valued was working hard, making money, keeping her head down, and that being a "good little follower" was important. So when she had recurring concerns about her manager, she hesitated to bring them up. "They wanted people just to do as they were told and not question anything. They didn't want employees' input."

Despite her reservations, Jennifer decided to talk to her CEO about her concerns with her manager. His suggestion was to bring it up with her manager's boss. And her manager's boss recommended she take up these concerns with her manager directly. She reluctantly agreed to set up a meeting with her manager.

"When I joined the call, my manager and her boss were on the screen. I knew at that moment that it was over," Jennifer says. "I was told that I was fired for lack of communication, poor leadership, and being a roadblock during group projects. The Zoom call lasted 1 minute and 15 seconds."

The CEO promised to call her later that evening, but never did. Instead, she was offered a severance package and allowed to keep her company computer. But she also had to sign an agreement that she wouldn't post on social media or say anything publicly about the company. She would later find out that this was not the typical practice when people were let go.

Ultimately, Jennifer says she feels the culture of the company did not value employee input and that someone like her, who was vocal about problems, was a threat. "I questioned everything about myself, along with how I knew myself as an employee. They truly made me feel like I was the problem." She sank into a deep depression that took months to recover from. That affected her search for a new job. Thankfully, today she has a new position elsewhere where she has learned that her work–life balance and input are both valued.

Culture is having an impact on employees every day. When you look at the results of research studies, it's important to remember the human beings behind the statistics.

Studying culture

Because culture is the root of behaviour within an organisation, it can influence every part of the business. Any efforts the organisation tries to make – from incorporating a new remote working policy to improving customer satisfaction levels – must explicitly address the cultural impact if the efforts are to be successful. It follows that when organisations get culture right, and intentions and behaviours are aligned, they are more likely to achieve their goals.

There are significant issues, however, in studying how culture is related to business results. The first issue is a lack of a shared understanding of how culture is defined and measured. If we can't agree on exactly what culture is and how it is measured, it is impossible to generalise about it. Similarly, culture research often highlights specific aspects of the culture; for example, cultures with high trust or cultures where employees feel valued and respected. In these examples, it's unclear whether what's important about culture is strategic alignment or the presence of specific cultural attributes (or a combination of attributes).

The uniqueness of each organisation's culture is also a barrier. Each organisation's ecosystem is unique and the way that their particular set of cultural attributes comes to life can vary so widely that it's hard to draw conclusions that other organisations can apply to their own situation.

That's one of the downsides of most culture books too.

They showcase one organisation's situation and readers want to take a culture cookie cutter back to their own organisation. But it just won't work. The importance of the unique context and organisational systems are why so much of the early work on culture was demonstrated through case studies, and the reason why there are fewer quantitative culture studies than you would expect.

Culture and business impact

As Jennifer's story demonstrates, culture has a real impact on human lives. It influences how people feel and think about an organisation, and in turn impacts their behaviours. And because of this feeling, thinking and behaving, culture will impact business results. Research indicates that organisational culture impacts a wide range of organisational results like retention, innovation, customer satisfaction and financial performance.

Some classic research on culture and business impact comes from a series of studies conducted by research professors John Kotter and James Heskett.[1] They found that cultures that were aligned with the business strategy and that adapted to changing market conditions (what they call "performance-enhancing cultures"), had significantly better revenue, employment, stock price and net income growth than firms without performance-enhancing cultures (see Figure 4).

Previously, most of the focus of culture research was on the strength of the culture. Kotter and Heskett showed that it's more important for the culture to be aligned with what the organisation is trying to achieve. They also showed that this process of connecting to strategy and adapting to external market conditions depends on effective leadership.

Figure 4: **The relationship between culture and business growth**

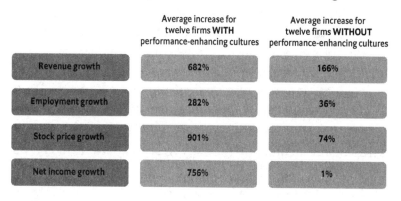

	Average increase for twelve firms **WITH** performance-enhancing cultures	Average increase for twelve firms **WITHOUT** performance-enhancing cultures
Revenue growth	682%	166%
Employment growth	282%	36%
Stock price growth	901%	74%
Net income growth	756%	1%

Source: J.P. Kotter and J.L. Heskett, *Corporate Culture and Performance* (New York: Free Press, 1992).

In another study, researchers from MIT/Sloan analysed 500 US companies and found that 21 of them were "culture champions", articulating and embodying their values.[2] The researchers found that over a five-year period, these 21 companies earned four times the returns of S&P 500 companies and twice the returns of NASDAQ companies.

Positive cultures tend to have positive work outcomes. But that doesn't mean all is well. Although leaders think that culture is important, many are not satisfied with progress in their own organisations. In a study of more than 1,300 North American CEOs and CFOs, 91% say culture is important to an organisation, and 92% say improving their company's culture will boost its value.[3] But only 16% of these executives believe that their own firm's culture is where it needs to be, with 69% indicating their firms' underinvestment in culture as a reason why. Some of the reasons for the underinvestment are impatient investors, inadequate governance structures and industry standards.

In this study, about 20% of the respondents indicate that their company's leadership works against the firm's culture being effective. (Remember: this is a survey of the top leaders, not employees.) This continuing disconnect between the perceived importance of culture and the lack of progress that organisations are making continues to astound me.

Although these research studies show the relationships between business results and culture, we still have a long way to go in our understanding of culture as a construct and therefore a long way to go in our ability to connect it with business outcomes. Many research studies rely on methodology that many consider to be more subjective (as in the Kotter and Heskett study, where CEOs were asked to rate their competitors' cultures as one of the key inputs) and many are about how employees feel about the culture (which is probably not a complete representation of what the culture really is).[4] Our understanding of culture continues to evolve. But in the meantime, culture is still impacting human beings – especially when that culture is toxic.

Toxic culture

Most of us have experienced first-hand the personal impact that culture can have on our lives. From simply being frustrated with certain aspects of our job to full-scale burnout that has serious physical and mental health implications, culture impacts us all. Toxic culture, a work environment characterised by negativity and dysfunction, is by far the strongest predictor of industry-adjusted attrition and is ten times more important than compensation in predicting turnover.[5] People are voting with their feet.

Just as having an aligned culture can positively differentiate one organisation from another, having a toxic culture can have such a significant negative impact on an organisation's reputation and brand that it can be almost impossible to recover. The organisation becomes labelled as a company no one wants to work for or buy products and services from. You don't have to look far to see these examples: talk to your neighbour or friends, and you can hear the impact that toxic cultures have had on real people.

Cynthia Montgomery and Ashley Whillans, professors at Harvard Business School, wrote a set of case studies that detail the horrific experiences of employees at France Telecom, where 19 employees died by suicide between 2006 and 2009 (and 12 others attempted suicide).[6] These were primarily older men who had been with the company for a long time.

One employee left a suicide note that said: "I am committing suicide because of my work at France Telecom, that's the only reason."

During that time, the company was shifting from being a monopoly to facing extreme pressure with outside companies entering the newly created cellular phone market. Company leaders were sinking the company into debt as they tried to purchase new technology and new competitors. There were massive layoffs. And for those who still had jobs, many were demoted to roles with lower status and less autonomy. Managers started monitoring employee behaviour and micromanaging. And they were asked by leaders to remove office chairs and use the word "if" whenever talking about their employees' future employment. Leaders gave bonuses to managers based on how many employees had left their teams.

A French court later found that the leaders of France Telecom had created a work culture of fear and harassment. Three of the top leaders were found guilty and sentenced to a year in prison, and four other leaders were found guilty of complicity. The company received a hefty fine. The court ruling stated that it was the "means chosen to reach the departures", not the layoffs themselves, that were illegal.

This is an extreme example. More usually, when you are in a toxic culture, it's obvious that it isn't right or healthy, but sometimes it's hard to put your finger on exactly what that means. Research from Massachusetts Institute of Technology suggests that toxic cultures in organisations conform to five cultural descriptors.[7]

1. **Disrespectful**. When a culture is disrespectful people don't feel that their time or efforts or even their existence is respected. This can result in people being interrupted, not being acknowledged, being humiliated or demeaned, the use of inappropriate language, harsh tones or shouting, gossip, being ignored and intimidation.

2. **Non-inclusive.** When a culture is non-inclusive, diverse perspectives and backgrounds are not represented and people do not feel welcomed, included or that they are being treated fairly.

3. **Unethical.** Unethical culture is characterised by a lack of integrity and dishonesty, often with a history of unethical behaviour or lack of compliance to rules and regulations.

4. **Cutthroat.** In cutthroat cultures, employees actively work against each other, with sabotage and feelings that people are "stabbing each other in the back".

5. **Abusive.** When a culture is abusive, people are routinely condescending, yelling and bullying. People (more often those in positions of power than frontline employees) use fear and intimidation to undermine or manipulate others, such as by being deceitful or overly political.

Each of these five areas is distinct but they often co-exist. Luckily, most companies aren't toxic; the research indicates that only approximately one in ten cultures qualifies. But if you are one of the not so lucky and have worked in a toxic culture, it's important to understand it.

Toxic culture and the dark triad of leadership

What's at the root of these toxic cultures? Research shows that leaders are the primary cause, closely followed by an organisation's social norms which, in many cases, were shaped by those leaders too.[8]

The most toxic leadership style is called the dark triad, based on the characteristics outlined in Figure 5.[9] The ominous name fits well with the unhealthy set of personality styles and behaviours that these leaders exhibit. Dark triad patterns have been found to be present in about 15% of leaders.[10]

Leaders with dark triad personalities are the ultimate gaslighters. They are manipulative, ruthless and crave power. They lack empathy and any sense of regret or conscience. They consider people to be a means to an end and are completely comfortable using others to get to the top.

Sounds awful, doesn't it? But often you don't realise you are working with dark triad leaders until after the fact. They

Figure 5: **Characteristics of the dark triad of leadership**

Machiavellianism	Narcissism	Psychopathy
Wheeler-dealer attitude	Grandiosity	Lacks remorse
Manipulates others	Ego reinforcement	Risk taker
Displays selfish behaviour	Strong emotional reactions	Displays reckless behaviour
Status driven	Self-enhancement	Low empathy
Distrusting of others	Sense of entitlement	Self-enhancement
Tendency towards duplicity	High self-worth	Antisocial

Source: D.L. Paulhus and K.M. Williams, "The dark triad of personality: narcissism, Machiavellianism and psychopathy", *Journal of Research in Personality*, 36(6) (2002), pp. 556–63.

can be so charming and charismatic that you don't realise what's happening. Their confidence and smoothness draw others to them, but these leaders manipulate and use others repeatedly, leaving a trail of discarded people behind them. When people are manipulated in this way, the foundation of trust is broken, and employees feel betrayed and damaged. As you can imagine, this kind of behaviour will cause deep harm to the culture.

Organisations tend to tolerate this kind of behaviour because these leaders often manage the perceptions of those "above" them very well, with boards not having easy access to the real experience that employees have. They often only see a highly charismatic leader who blames others for organisational failures.

Sometimes these leaders are moved to other departments or organisations, often under the guise of being top performers. Shuffling toxic leaders sends a clear message to employees that the organisation isn't living its values and doesn't care about the values either.

If leaders are primary drivers of the culture, it's clearly important that they are chosen wisely and held accountable for the culture they create. Leaders who exhibit the dark triad can have a significant negative impact on organisational culture, particularly in terms of trust, collaboration and employee well-being. Organisations should be mindful of these traits when selecting and evaluating leaders, and should work to promote a positive, values-driven culture that supports the well-being and success of all employees.

Towards positive cultures at work

Now that you know what makes up a toxic culture, let's look at the kind of positive culture that organisations should look to create.

A more positive culture:

- is based on mutual trust (the employees trust the organisation and the organisation trusts the employees)
- is aligned with the strategy
- supports engagement
- can adapt to changing conditions.

Toxic cultures are poisonous and soul sucking. The opposite is life-giving. The organisational tree analogy is still relevant. The roots of our tree should be fully alive, growing. The culture should be thriving.

But thriving cultures rarely happen on their own. Organisations must be intentional about the cultures they create and how they are aligned to the business strategy and the market. They also have to make sure the experience of culture aligns with the intention.

One of the most fundamental aspects of a thriving culture is trust. Research by Gallup indicates that when employees trust leaders, they have higher levels of engagement.[11] And a study of 6,300 Holiday Inn employees found that hotels where managers followed through on their promises and had behavioural integrity were more profitable.[12]

Trust is about whether two parties have the best interests of each other in mind. In the employer/employee relationship, trust is multifaceted. People can have trust in their managers, in the strategic direction of the organisation and in the organisation itself.[13]

Consider these different aspects of trust by asking yourself the following questions about where you work.

Manager trust is the trust people have in their own managers.

- Do managers treat team members fairly?
- Do managers consider employees' needs when making decisions about the business?
- Do managers put the company's needs ahead of their own desires?

Strategic trust is the trust people have in leaders to make the right strategic decisions.

- Do they have confidence in the direction the company is headed?
- Do they believe the leaders have the vision and competence to set the right course, allocate resources intelligently, fulfill the mission and help the company succeed?

Organisational trust is the trust people have in the organisation itself rather than in any individual.

- Are processes well designed, consistent and fair?
- Does the organisation make good on its promises?
- Are leaders overall credible? Do they mean what they say? Is what they say true?
- Are leaders overall ethical in their business practices?
- Are people treated with respect?
- Are people's views and ideas included?
- Are they treated fairly, regardless of position?

Trust is the foundation for a thriving culture, one many of us can take for granted. But when trust is broken (like when you have dark triad leadership), it is very apparent. As this quote, often attributed to Warren Buffett, puts so well, "Trust is like the air we breathe. When it's present, nobody really notices. But when it's absent, everybody notices."

Fortunately, many of us do experience thriving cultures. Ashley has been a nurse for 17 years, specialising in pediatric care. Eventually her skillset led her to a position at one of the United States' major children's hospitals. She has been at this job for several years, including through the covid-19 pandemic, and has no plans to leave.

"I had one job a few years ago that I felt valued at, but not for long," she says. "But this hospital is different, and they are very understanding about family and work–life balance."

As a single mother, she says this has made a huge difference to her. In her role, her job responsibilities are flexible, as she has a work-from-home position reviewing charts. "If I tell them I'm leaving for an hour this afternoon to take my child to the doctor, they're fine with it," Ashley says. "I can do what I want, how I want, as long as I get my work done."

For Ashley, the company's intentional focus on creating a positive culture has affected her decision to stay. At one point, she considered a change for various personal reasons and for a different routine. However, everything about how the organisation treats nurses is better than anywhere she has worked before or anywhere she has considered. They include employees when major decisions (eg, on pay scales) are being made, and they actively work to make policies reinforce positive behaviours, rather than being punitive. Pay and benefits are good, and the hospital is proactive about being inclusive to LGBTQIA+ and racially diverse employees.

"When my senior director sensed I was looking to leave and reached out to me personally about it, she told me how much I was needed and that I would be missed," Ashley relates. She says that solidified her decision to stay.

And that means that a seasoned, quality nurse is remaining with a hospital at a time when hospitals are losing more nurses than ever. Ashley's very human example shows the impact that a thriving culture can have.

Remember

1. Because culture is difficult to define and is unique to each organisation, it is difficult to study.
2. But research indicates that culture is statistically related to business results.
3. Toxic cultures are caused primarily by toxic leaders, and can have an extremely negative impact on human beings and organisations.
4. Organisations can create thriving cultures if they build trust, are intentional, and work to make sure their cultural intentions are aligned with their employees' cultural experiences.

I have now set the stage by describing what culture is, how important the experience of culture is, and why it matters. In the next chapter, I begin to describe the journey of understanding culture evolution, so that more of us can experience a thriving culture.

PART 2

Evolving culture

Overview

Now that we have defined culture, uncovered many of its complexities and discussed why it matters so much to people and to businesses, the next part of this book covers how to change culture for the better.

In Chapter 4, I look into how to know when an organisation needs to change its culture, including what signs to look for and whether the organisation is ready to take on culture work. Before embarking on the difficult journey of evolving culture, there must be a clear starting point – the type of culture work depends on where the culture is now. In this chapter I also introduce the Intentional Culture Circle, an approach that helps to operationalise the potentially overwhelming and ambiguous nature of culture change.

In Chapters 5 and 6, I further discuss the Intentional Culture Circle, explaining each of the components and how to put each of them into practice. The Intentional Culture Circle comprises eight elements divided into two sections.

Chapter 5 focuses on setting the stage for intentional culture and encompasses the first four elements: Vision, Behaviours, Education and Accountability.

The second section of the Intentional Culture Circle, detailed in Chapter 6, is dedicated to bringing the culture to life and includes the other four elements: Champions, Communications, Experiences and Systems.

In Chapter 7, the last chapter of Part 2, I dig into the important subject of organisational power and its impact on shaping the culture within an organisation. This chapter emphasises the significance of understanding power dynamics in an organisation and incorporating these power dynamics into our understanding of culture and how it evolves. I argue that power, while often associated with negative connotations, can also be a constructive force, unifying and inspiring people to work together to help achieve an organisation's goals, strategy and purpose.

4

Are you ready to change?

Oti-Yeboah Complex Limited (OYCL) is a wood-processing mill, located in Sunyani, Ghana, and has a workforce of about 1,600 employees. Initially, OYCL operated as a sawmill, producing processed wood products for both domestic and international markets. However, because of the depletion of its forest and lack of raw materials, it transitioned to producing plywood. This change had a significant impact on the company, affecting its strategy, structure, culture, technology and work processes. Employees faced new roles, potential redundancy and increased responsibilities.[1]

This transformation triggered resistance from employees who were uncertain about the changes and concerned about their job security. Consequently, the organisation experienced a series of employee strikes, boycotts and lockouts, resulting in production stoppages. The period marked a challenging transition for OYCL as it navigated the complexities of change.

Rosemond Boohene and Asamoah Williams, professors at the University of Cape Coast, Ghana, sought to understand the factors that led some employees to be more resistant than others to the changes at OYCL. Resistance to change is the set of negative attitudes, thoughts and behaviours people have about impending change. The researchers found that a lack of employee participation in decision making, lack of trust in management, lack of motivation and poor communication were the strongest contributors to people's resistance. These factors created a perfect storm that made a difficult transition even more challenging.

Some organisations seek to squelch the resistance people have to change – to tell or convince people that they should not have these negative attitudes, thoughts and behaviours. Others see that seeking to understand the resistance is a way to improve their approach, such as how the change is communicated and how people participate in the change process.

Other organisations refuse to acknowledge that they need to change, even in the face of harsh reality. An awful analogy comes from a saying from horse trainers: "If the horse you're riding dies, get off." Many organisations don't face the reality that they need to change horses; instead, they buy a stronger whip, try a new bridle, switch riders, arrange to visit a site where other organisations ride their dead horses more efficiently or complain about the state of horses these days.[2] You get the point. It's difficult for organisations to realise that they need to change, let alone change in ways that bring people along with them. But change is a requirement for organisations to survive. And culture is one of the most important aspects – if not the most important aspect – that needs to change.

That's where culture evolution comes in.

Culture evolution is the process of intentionally developing specific aspects of an organisation's norms, values and beliefs. Sometimes it's obvious when an organisation needs to evolve its culture: business results are suffering, employees are leaving. But other times, it requires more investigation.

Signs your culture needs to evolve

Apart from when it is painfully obvious, how else do you know when the organisation needs to do culture work? Here are some signs to look out for.

Use the data

Look out for trends and patterns in any data that you have, for example, employee surveys, exit interviews, customer complaints and online reviews.

If the same things come up time and again, it could mean that they're being addressed at a climate level, and you may need to dig deeper to look at them from a cultural perspective. Let's say your employee survey results across multiple teams tell you that cross-group collaboration is low; despite efforts to build skills to help employees collaborate, results still haven't changed. It would be important to dig into what is fundamentally valued in the culture that might be reinforcing individual performance (or even reinforcing competitiveness) between employees. This might be why your efforts on the climate level are not gaining any traction.

Strategy change

Another time to focus on culture is when your organisation is going through a change in business strategy or having difficulties executing a business strategy. It may be that there is a fundamental culture issue that is an obstacle to what you are trying to achieve strategically.

Culture needs to evolve if your organisation is in the process of acquiring another company or has a history of mergers/acquisitions. Culture clash between the acquiring and acquired companies is one of the biggest reasons that mergers and acquisitions fail. But most organisations are still not investing in culture discovery and integration when acquiring other companies.

Recruitment and retention difficulties

Your culture might need more attention if people are leaving your organisation in higher numbers than in the past (or if the highest performing employees are leaving) or if you are having difficulty attracting new candidates to your organisation. Even if the culture isn't toxic, it can still be one that isn't thriving – and employees and candidates will vote with their feet.

Lack of employee participation and engagement

If people are showing signs of disengagement – for example, no longer attending company/all-hands meetings or no longer asking questions – this may be an indication of withdrawal from the culture and a precursor to people leaving. It's another early sign that you might need to work on your culture.

Disconnects between leaders and employees

Another big tell is a lack of connection and alignment between leaders and employees, even though there's been lots of communication. For example, employees might refer to the company and company leadership as "they" (rather than saying "we" or "us"). Or leaders have an us versus them mentality when referring to people in the organisation, consistently blaming the workforce or a lack of talent for not achieving business results.

Another indicator is when leaders do not engage with or listen to employees, with little or no empathy with what they are going through.

If leaders are not role models for the culture, if they blame others rather than taking ownership themselves, it's a sign that the culture (and the leaders) need to evolve.

Is your organisation ready to change?

It's one thing to know that you have a culture problem. It's a completely different thing to know if the organisation is ready to change.

Most change management models are based on the idea that change is a process and that there are natural stages that human beings go through as they move through that process. In organisations, the more you can acknowledge and proactively address those natural stages, the more likely everyone will come along on the "change journey" and be more satisfied with the changes you are making.

For example, Kotter's 8-Step Change Model is a structured approach to managing organisational change.[3]

1. **Establish a sense of urgency.** Begin by creating a compelling reason for change. This step aims to convince stakeholders that change is necessary.

2. **Form a powerful coalition.** Assemble a team of influential individuals who can lead the change effort effectively.

3. **Create a vision for change.** Develop a clear and concise vision that outlines what the future will look like after the change is implemented.

4. **Communicate the vision.** Share the vision with the entire organisation to ensure that everyone understands and embraces it.

5. **Empower broad-based action.** Remove obstacles and encourage employees to take action to realise the vision.

6. **Generate short-term wins.** Celebrate early successes to build momentum and boost morale.

7. **Consolidate gains and produce more change.** Use momentum from early wins to tackle more significant changes.

8. **Anchor new approaches in the culture.** Ensure that the new way of working becomes the norm by embedding it in the organisation's culture. (Note that this change model talks about embedding the new change into the culture; many others do not.)

The Kübler-Ross Change Curve, also known as the Change Transition Curve, was developed by psychiatrist Elisabeth Kübler-Ross and is another change model used by many organisations.[4] It describes the emotional journey that individuals often go through when dealing with significant change.

The curve typically includes five stages.

1. **Denial.** Initially, people may deny that the change is happening or resist accepting it.

2. **Anger.** As the reality of change sets in, individuals may become angry or frustrated about the situation.

3. **Bargaining.** People may attempt to negotiate or find ways to minimise the impact of the change.

4. **Depression.** Feelings of sadness and hopelessness can arise as individuals come to terms with the change.

5. **Acceptance.** Ultimately, individuals accept the new reality and begin to adapt and move forward.

Another commonly used change model is called the ADKAR Model, developed by Prosci.[5] ADKAR is an acronym representing five key elements necessary for successful change.

1. **Awareness.** Understand why the change is necessary and the implications it has for individuals and the organisation.
2. **Desire.** Develop a personal motivation or desire to support and engage in the change.
3. **Knowledge.** Acquire the knowledge and skills needed to implement the change effectively.
4. **Ability.** Gain the ability to apply the knowledge and skills in practice.
5. **Reinforcement.** Ensure that the change is sustained over time through rewards, recognition and adjustments as necessary.

All three change models address the process of change in organisations, but they have distinct focuses and applications. Kotter's model emphasises the organisational aspect of change, offering a structured approach for leaders to guide their teams through change initiatives. Kübler-Ross's model focuses on the emotional journey that individuals experience during change, providing insight into the human side of transitions. The ADKAR model centres on individual change readiness and personal adaptation to new circumstances, with a strong emphasis on knowledge, motivation and skills.

These models emphasise different areas, but they all share the overarching goal of facilitating successful organisational change. Organisations often use a combination of these models to address both the human and organisational aspects of change, acknowledging that change involves both structured processes and individual reactions.

The three models also highlight the significance of individual readiness and the need for planning and communication during the change process. They emphasise the importance of building awareness, understanding and buy-in among the people involved. They also recognise the importance of reinforcement and sustaining change over the long term and how important it is to embed new behaviours and practices to ensure lasting change.

When working to change culture, deciding which model to use is not as important as just *using* a model. And, of course, that model should consider that change is a process that requires intention and time and that you shouldn't expect the acceptance of change to be linear or without challenges. Remember: people and organisations do not simply transition from one state to another instantaneously. Acknowledging and addressing the psychological and emotional aspects of change is critical.

Change management is not enough

Culture change absolutely requires change management: the process you use and what steps you take can go a long way to addressing the natural stages you expect employees to go through. But there are other factors to bear in mind too.

Because culture is influenced by power (of which more in Chapter 7), the highest levels of leadership must be the primary voices in any culture evolution efforts. And they can't just be talking heads or going through the motions – there must be an authentic commitment from these leaders to do the culture work. These leaders also need to be respected by employees to be able to have the influence that's required for culture evolution. This is different from simply changing a software system, for example. In that case, it might be helpful to have the CEO support the efforts, but it is probably not critical that they do. With culture work, it is.

This doesn't mean that others in the organisation can't

also be culture change drivers, but without the CEO and other leaders being involved it will be difficult for the change to be implemented and almost impossible for the change to stick. Imagine a situation where a director led the company's culture efforts and the CEO was supportive of the work but was passive (and was definitely not the culture "voice" to the rest of the company). This work could move forward and some progress could be made, but the message this sends to employees is that there are other things that are more important to the company than culture. And whatever it is that the CEO does decide to voice to the rest of the company will be considered more important.

Another important consideration is the state of the organisation's business strategy, mission, vision and purpose. Starting on the journey of culture evolution requires a thorough analysis of the organisation's business strategy so that the critical alignment between strategy and culture is clear. Is the business strategy clearly articulated? Has it changed since it was last articulated? What has changed and why? Is everyone clear about what's changed?

The culture work will only be as solid as the strategic foundation it is built on.

A useful way of thinking about culture change is to think about *organisational-level* habit change. The organisation, over time, has got into habits or ways of doing things and some of these habits may no longer be serving the organisation well anymore. So how do you change the habits you no longer want or need? By applying the ideas of habit change to organisations.

The takeaways from James Clear's book *Atomic Habits* align nicely with this approach.[6] Rather than focusing on individuals, improving systems – such as the leadership system, the learning system, the incentive system or customer service system – is more likely to encourage new ways of doing things. When the old organisational level habits are replaced, it's more likely that change will occur.

Changing who you are also starts by changing what you do. Are you a runner first and then you start running? Or is it because you have the habit of running that you are a runner? Culture change is similar. When you put the new cultural behaviours (or culture habits) into place to become who you want to become, you're more likely to prevail. One of the most straightforward ways to change organisational habits is to change what the organisation does.

Culture work is personal

When working on culture change, be ready for pushback, conflict and challenges. Many culture beliefs are so deeply rooted that questioning them can feel threatening to some people. And when people feel threatened, they often lash out and push back.

Culture work can get heated, sometimes in unexpected ways and at unexpected times. Those who do culture work have to be scientists, investigators, anthropologists, storytellers, artists, coaches, therapists and relationship experts all rolled into one. And they must have courage and patience too.

Because culture feels both personal and deeply rooted, it is important to have a clear "why" for the culture work. There needs to be a sense of urgency and a clear, meaningful reason for things to change. That's why it's so important to draw explicit connections with the organisation's strategy and purpose. Culture work should always be focused on solving business problems.

To help address these issues, there's a simple but important approach I like to take called "hearts and minds". The idea is that in addition to being logical and systematic, it's just as important to connect with people on an emotional level.

Helping employees understand why and how the culture needs to change means working with people at the emotional level (hearts), cognitive level (minds), and behavioural levels (how both hearts and minds manifest).

Know where you are starting from

You have to know where you are starting from. Take a look again at the grid of articulated and experienced culture in Figure 1, Chapter 2 (page 37). If your organisation has articulated the culture it wants and the experience of culture is happening or starting to happen, then the organisation is probably already down the path of being intentional about culture.

But if the organisation is in any other quadrant, moving forward with being intentional about culture isn't the next step. Instead, you'll need to make sure that this work is a priority and that leaders are committed to moving forward.

To know if your organisation is ready to take on culture change, look at these three key tests.

There is a "burning platform" or a compelling "why".

The CEO and leadership team see culture work as critical to the success of the company and are ready to do the work *and* ready to be the voice of the culture work.

There is a shared understanding that the work is a long-term commitment that requires fortitude.

Let's talk through an example where an organisation has a new CEO who has a vision for a very different business model for the organisation. This new business model requires significant innovation and an increased focus on technology, which was significantly different from the previous model. Test #1: ✓.

The new CEO was aware that there was a need for significant culture work. In fact, it was part of why she was hired. In her short tenure she has already spoken to the leadership team about how transforming the culture is the most important part of their leadership agenda. In her first talk with all employees on her first day, she acknowledged how far the organisation has come and how great the culture has been, but also that she is excited for the future and how the culture is going to evolve to help the organisation be successful. She committed to monthly talks about her vision for the organisation, especially to talk about how the culture needs to evolve. Test #2: ✓.

Finally, the new CEO has set the expectations with all employees, the leadership team and the board that she understands that this important work won't happen overnight, in fact it will take years to accomplish. But she is in it for the long haul and hopes that they are too. Test #3: ✓.

With these three foundational pieces in place, the organisation is ready to start the culture work.

Types of culture work

Given that organisations are unique and will start on culture work from very different places, there are also different types of culture work that an organisation might need (see Figure 6).

- You may simply be trying to understand the current culture (**culture investigation**).
- You might be trying to create or form your aspirational culture (think of start-ups). That's **cultural formation**.
- You may want to work out how to compare the current culture with the aspirational culture and close the gaps between the two – this is **culture transformation**. It implies an important shift in the culture that the

Figure 6: **Types of culture work**

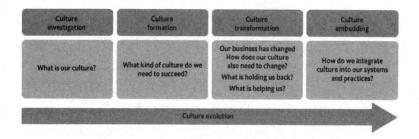

organisation is trying to make and that it is necessary to move *from* a specific kind of culture *to* a different kind of culture.

- The culture work may involve making the culture come to life throughout the organisation, ensuring that the experience of culture is woven throughout the organisation. This is called **culture embedding**.

Make sure you are clear about the questions you are trying to answer. No matter the type of culture work you are doing, you must be intentional about it. As you move further down the path in the culture work towards culture embedding, that intentionality becomes even more important.

Intentional Culture Circle

Even when an organisation knows that it needs to be more intentional about its culture, it can be hard to know what to do next. There is often a disconnect between culture change in theory and what really happens in organisations.

That's what the Intentional Culture Circle (Figure 7) is designed to do: provide clarity about how to go about culture work on the ground. It gives organisations a simple approach to help make culture come to life.

Figure 7: **Intentional Culture Circle**

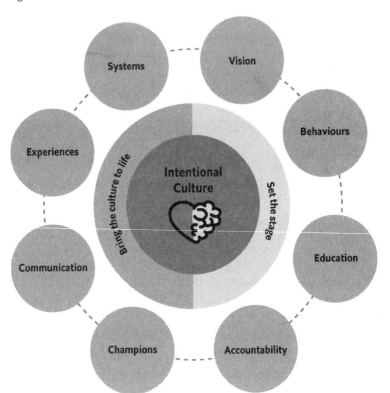

This circle has eight elements, divided into two sections.

The first section, described in Chapter 5, explores how to set the stage for being intentional about culture. This incorporates the first four elements of the Intentional Culture Circle.

Vision. Determining the culture the organisation needs in order to achieve its strategy.

Behaviours. Articulating what the culture the organisation needs looks like in action.

Education. How everyone (current and future) in the

organisation comes to learn about the culture the organisation aspires to.

Accountability. Creating clear accountability for being intentional about culture, which involves having clear metrics and responsible parties for culture evolution.

The second section of the Intentional Culture Circle, described in Chapter 6, is about bringing the culture to life. This incorporates the other four elements.

Champions. Ensuring that other people in the organisation – not just leaders – are active drivers of the culture.

Communications. A regular and consistent "drumbeat" about the culture the organisation is aspiring to.

Experiences. Intentional and curated ways in which people come together and experience the culture.

Systems. How systems, policies and processes align with, and support, the culture you want to create.

In my experience, although people in an organisation can be clear that the culture needs to change, it can be a daunting task – so daunting that it never gets addressed. This model helps to operationalise something that can feel so abstract that it can feel impossible. Think of this model as a way of making the abstraction real, so you can start working on creating better cultures.

Remember

1. Being intentional about culture is not only possible, it's critical to organisational success and people's experience at work.

2. Being intentional requires a hearts and minds approach.

3. There are many kinds of culture work; it's important to be clear what the questions and goals of the work are before you start.

4. Embarking on culture evolution isn't for the faint of heart. But using business strategy as the frame and the Intentional Culture Circle as a guide, it is a do-able and worthwhile pursuit.

Now that you have discovered if you are ready to change your culture, let's start using the Intentional Culture Circle to set the stage for culture evolution.

5

Intention: Setting the stage for culture evolution

Jay Tuli, the president of Leader Bank, has learned the importance of culture by starting backwards. He was laser focused on achieving results, especially expansion and growth, in the bank that his father started in 2002. And he learned, over time, that one of the best ways to get those results was to be intentional about culture, to make the work environment better and more sustainable for everyone who works there. "If you want to achieve results, a talented team is the way to get there."

During the financial crisis of 2008, many banks were failing and going under. And so there were a lot of experienced and talented people who he was able to hire at his smaller bank – simply because his bank was still standing and financially healthy. Jay felt grateful that this talent seemed to fall into the bank's lap. But now that his bank had this great talent, how was it going to keep them? Jay realised that he needed to create the conditions at Leader Bank so that people would not want to leave.

It took a while for him to work it out, especially as he hadn't had any formal training or exposure to how to be intentional about culture. He thought that a focus on culture was only for big companies that had extra time and money on their hands. But Jay had big goals and realised that he needed to find out which levers to pull to achieve his goals. That's when he started getting really clear about a focus on culture.

Jay and the other leaders at Leader Bank started by creating a shared vision of what the culture needed to be, which they call the Leader Bank Way. The Leader Bank Way focuses on being client obsessed; always looking for ways to get better, to give clients new solutions and to keep their own egos out of the way. This approach also encourages the development of new products and experimentation with new offerings. And they connect these kinds of behaviours to the bank's economic model. Jay and his colleagues make culture a natural part of the language that everyone at Leader Bank uses in their daily work.

And their culture journey has not ended. Jay is clear that culture work is ongoing. "Culture is either getting better or getting worse. So you have to keep evolving and growing it. It's not something you do and then you are done. It's like working out. You have to keep working out otherwise your muscles atrophy."

So how do you keep building your culture muscles?

That's what the Intentional Culture Circle (Figure 7) is designed to do: provide clarity about how to go about culture work on the ground. It gives organisations a simple approach to help make culture come to life.

The eight elements of the circle fall into two categories. The first four elements are about setting the stage for more intentional culture and are described later in this chapter. The other four elements are about bringing the culture to life and are described in the next chapter.

Figure 7a: **Intentional Culture Circle**

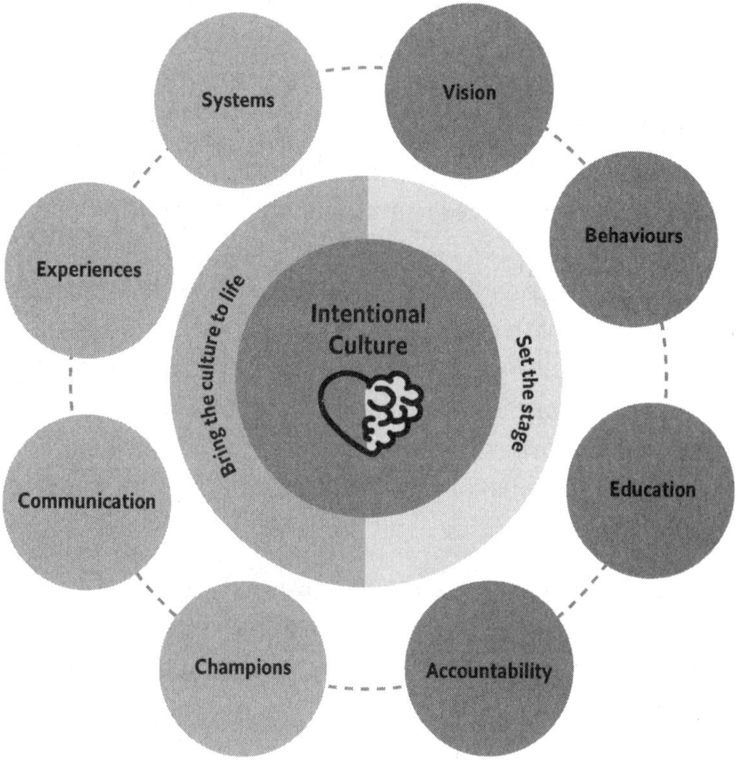

Step 1. Culture vision

Creating a shared vision for culture is no easy task. A vision is aspirational and inspirational, but a shared vision requires you to bring others along in the journey of creating it. That's important because it sets the stage and articulates what the organisation should be striving for.

The central idea is to be clear about the kind of behaviours you want people to exhibit and what kind of organisation you're trying to create. This articulation should make it clear why culture matters so much to the business and how important everyone in the organisation is in making it a force for good.

Understand your current culture and where you want and need to go next

The process starts with a clear understanding of what the current culture is. There are multiple approaches you can take.

You could license an off-the-shelf culture assessment or work with a consulting firm that has its own proprietary measure. Alternatively, you (or a consultant) could conduct your own research – in a series of culture workshops, perhaps – asking everyone in the organisation to describe how the culture really works.

Sample questions for the culture workshops might include the following.

- If you were describing our organisation's culture to a neighbour or a new friend, what words would you use?
- What are the three words that you think best describe our organisation's current culture?
- What is special about our culture?
- What kinds of behaviour gets recognised and rewarded here?
- What kinds of people get promoted?
- If someone from the outside came in and observed our culture for a day, what do you think they would say?
- How is our organisation's culture different from the last place you worked? How is it similar?
- What are our organisation's values?
- How are our values used in the day-to-day work with employees?

- Are our values part of the language that employees use in their daily work? How so?

- How do our values show up in the work itself? How do you see them being used to make decisions?

- From a culture perspective, what do you think is holding this organisation back from achieving its mission/ purpose/strategy?

- From a culture perspective, what do you think is helping this organisation in achieving its mission/purpose/strategy?

If you already have a set of values, you can ask people how well the values describe your current culture and the extent to which the values are demonstrated in practice. Remember: it's helpful to understand culture at the attribute level (the discrete elements of the culture like integrated, secretive and caring described in Chapter 1) and also how the attributes work together to describe the organisation's particular culture.

Develop the "aspire to" culture

The next stage is to determine the culture you need to have in future to achieve your strategy or purpose.

Typically, this discussion starts at a leadership or broader management level, and the frame (that is, how you set up the discussion) for this part of the work is critical. The shared vision must have a **deep and explicit connection with what the business is trying to achieve**. That can be in the form of the business strategy, vision, mission or purpose. For example, take a credit union whose purpose is to help members build their financial health. This type of purpose would indicate different cultural attributes (like support, education and a focus on the long-term) to those of a bank focused more on maximising its own profits.

Because culture is an enduring, long-term construct, it's important to connect it to longer-term business goals, like vision or purpose, especially if the strategy is designed to be the focus only for the next year. Sometimes business strategy can be too short term for the connection with the culture that you're trying to articulate.

In addition to this strategic frame, it is important to be clear about what problems you are trying to solve with the culture work. For example, are you concerned that people:

- aren't as innovative as they need to be?
- don't feel enough ownership and accountability?
- aren't providing good customer service?
- aren't working in a system that is operationally sound?
- are working in silos?

Strategic alignment and a clear sense of business problems help to build the case for why culture needs to change.

Take a software company that is struggling to get and keep customers. The underlying business idea is still relevant and there is still a market for what the company is selling, but the product has not evolved and is not attracting users. The leadership team decides that they must become much more connected to current and potential users and redevelop their product. It is also clear that the culture needs to change to reflect this increased focus on the product and its users. They develop a strategic plan for how they will become more product- and user-focused as well as a strategic vision for the aspirational culture that needs to go hand in hand with this shift in business strategy.

Analyse the gaps between current and "aspire to" culture

Armed with an understanding of the current culture and a sense of the culture the organisation needs to have to be successful, you can then compare the two. Looking at them side by side you start to see:

- which aspects of the current culture should be **maintained** (these aspects are still helping the organisation achieve its goals)
- which need to be **changed** or moved away from (these culture attributes are hindering the organisation from achieving its goals)
- which aspects are **new** to the organisation. This list may be long at first, but with further discussion you can prioritise what should be included in the shared vision.

This will enable you to create a culture vision that's ready to be communicated and tested.

Articulate the shared vision

At this stage, it's time to articulate the shared vision that has been developed of the culture. It's important to deliver this articulation in a format that is authentic and human, ideally in a face-to-face meeting (and definitely not in just an email). This shared vision should tell the story of where you want to move *from* and *to* and why this change is so important to the business. It also should outline the culture journey ahead and how people will continue to have opportunities to learn and engage along the way.

There are many ways to do this effectively. Some organisations create a culture playbook, a culture deck, a leadership video or a special intranet site. This shared vision should be developed over time, making sure that everyone in the organisation feels involved. Leaders should spend time listening to the perspectives of others across the organisation, making improvements to the culture vision as they go. Some leaders do this through a culture listening "tour" where they spend time with employees and get their perspectives on the ideas they have for the culture vision. Others offer sessions (formal and informal) where people can ask questions and dig deeper. It's important to give people the time to process what the change means to them and to their teams. Ask them to give examples of when they see the aspirational culture playing out and when they don't.

It's also important to ensure that you document the culture vision so that it can be repeatedly shared in consistent ways to both existing employees and new employees. This documentation can be through narrative, presentation, video or a combination. What's important is that you tell the story of the culture, including why it matters and what you need from people to make it real.

At Leader Bank, Jay Tuli has created a document that articulates the shared culture vision called the Brand Bible. As he describes: "This is not a squishy document. This is real. And I say this to the team, I say this to anybody. 'In business there are 50 different ways you can make money, but this is the way *we* make money.'"

You will start to know that the way that you've defined and articulated the culture vision is working when people connect with and want to be a part of the new culture. The shared culture vision sets the stage for being intentional about culture because it paints an aspirational and inspirational picture and articulates the "why" for the work ahead.

It's the starting point for making a connection with people in how they think about the company, how they feel about the company, and how they behave (and interact with other people) while at the company.

Cultural evolution needs both hearts and minds: it has to be based on solid business foundations while also addressing the emotions and behaviours of the people who work there.

Step 2. Behaviours

Once the shared vision of the culture is understood and articulated, the next stage is to identify the behaviours that will underpin it. Everyone must understand what the aspirational culture looks like in action, and what the expectations are for their own behaviour and interactions with others. This step makes the culture vision "real" – people can start to see what it means and how they need to act to be aligned.

Many organisations skip this step. It seems too detailed, prescriptive and hard to articulate. And because leaders are driving this process, I see many shutting down to this idea because they don't want to get that tactical. But keeping the culture work at the vision level doesn't make it come to life. Creating clear behavioural expectations creates clarity. If you are asking people to behave differently, it is critical that you can share what that looks like. It's also critical that leaders and managers model these key behaviours themselves.

Clarity is kindness. People appreciate knowing what is expected of them. And managers also appreciate having this tool to talk with employees about performance expectations and career growth. These behaviours can be powerful for career and development discussions. They offer a language to talk about what success looks like. I call these behaviours "values in action".

When developing behavioural expectations, it's important to be thorough, but also simple, which is no easy feat. Balance having enough detail about what people need to do, but make sure that the entire list is not overwhelming.

Values in action: an example

Here is an example of values in action for employees, focusing specifically on one value related to learning and growth.

In this organisation, we:

1. Embrace lifelong learning, practise self-reflection, demonstrate a desire to learn, and look for and participate in formal and informal learning opportunities.
2. Share what we know with others and embrace opportunities to learn from others.
3. Encourage the learning and growth of others.
4. Take on complex problems and are eager to find solutions.
5. Adjust to changes and new ways of doing things, even if they are outside of our comfort zone.
6. Ask for and act on feedback.
7. Provide thoughtful and actionable feedback to others.
8. Accept feedback; do not take constructive feedback personally, but instead as an opportunity to grow.
9. Admit when mistakes are made and learn from them.

When I work on these values in action, I like to create three sets of behaviours: one for employees (like those listed above), one for managers, and one for leaders (especially in larger organisations where these roles are more explicit and defined). With these three sets of behaviours, the organisation can show a progression and a connection between all levels.

And this progression can also demonstrate a career path from employees to managers to leaders.

In the example above, I would also develop a set of behaviours for managers that describe how they can support their employees to focus on their growth and development. For example, how managers coach others to help them learn, how they provide constructive feedback to team members, and how they help team members learn from the mistakes they make. For leaders (typically defined as managers of managers), I would develop a set of behaviours that describe how they can support the organisation to focus on growth and development. For example, how leaders create systems and process that support employee growth, how they anticipate future trends and opportunities for the organisation, and how they create a vision to ensure the organisation can innovate and grow to meet those opportunities.

Creating these behaviours means involving people in carrying out a range of roles in articulating what they look like, using language that is accessible and relevant. They should not be mandated from above but developed through discovery and exploration throughout the organisation, typically through focus groups. This not only helps to gather information, but also involvement in crafting the behaviours boosts understanding and improves buy-in. The behaviours should be descriptive, but as succinct as possible.

It may take some iteration, but it's important to land on a set of behaviours that describe the aspects of the aspirational culture in a way that is unique and appropriate to the organisation, and clear and actionable for everyone.

Step 3. Education

When you've articulated the shared vision of the culture and you've created behavioural expectations, you've painted a picture of what culture should look like in your organisation. Ideally, people will be emotionally connected and inspired about what the culture could be, and you've described the aspirational culture in behavioural terms. The next step is to make sure you're educating people about what that culture is.

Remember: people learn about culture over time, through many different sources. Intentional culture education is a way to formalise that learning, and it encourages people to have a growth mindset (a belief that a person's abilities aren't innate or unchangeable but can be improved through effort and learning). Everyone needs to fully grasp the "aspire to" culture, why it matters, and how it has evolved over time. An important part of this educational component is storytelling – about the company's origin, purpose and current and "aspire to" culture – using compelling and human examples.

In some ways, culture education is relatively easy because you have the content in the shared culture vision and in behavioural expectations. What's hard about education is how you embed it to make it repeatable and scalable. Culture education needs to be accessible, consistent and ongoing.

Accessible

Accessible means culture education meets people where they are. Culture education should be externally available to your potential candidates, customers and partners too. They should easily be able to learn what your organisation stands for and how people are expected to behave with each other. Once candidates become employees, they should have easy access to more detail about the culture. And it shouldn't stop there:

culture education should be a recurring part of all meetings, town halls (company-wide meetings) and formal development programmes.

Organisations should use a variety of channels to ensure that their culture is communicated effectively to everyone. This can include email, meetings, workshops, training sessions or internal communication platforms.

And remember: education isn't one-way – there's a lot that an organisation can learn from its people about culture. Encouraging employees to provide feedback and engage in discussions about company culture can help foster a sense of ownership and accountability. This can also help identify areas where values may not be consistently applied across the organisation. There are many forms this kind of feedback can take. Weaving questions into your employee surveys, conducting separate pulse surveys specifically asking about the culture, conducting focus groups about the culture and incorporating breakout sessions into company meetings are all ways to gather this type of feedback.

Consistent

The culture message should be consistent. The shared vision and the behaviours address some of that consistency, but it's also important that anyone delivering the culture education understands how and why the culture work was conducted. At one company where I worked, the onboarding instructor said: "Oh yeah, here are our values. I don't know how or why they were created, but you are supposed to memorise them." You can imagine the impact that had on us as new employees on our first day of work.

Ongoing

Culture education should be ongoing. Most organisations understand that they should talk about culture during onboarding, but that's as far as it goes. But you need to keep going with both new and established employees to make sure the messages hit home.

It's important to make time and space for people to learn about the culture. One thing I see and hear from leaders is frustration when people don't do things or act in ways that they'd hoped. And my first questions to them are: have you put those things down on paper or spoken to employees about them? Have you spent time teaching them? Have you set clear expectations? That's what these first three steps of the Intentional Culture Circle are intended to do. They set the stage for clarity so that employees have what they need to help the culture come to life. Without that, there's no room for a leader to complain. It's their job to make sure they create clarity around the culture they need to have.

Jay Tuli at Leader Bank understood the assignment to make the implicit, explicit. "Without knowing the rich history and the habits and the why behind how we do certain things, team members will not be in sync with everyone else and they might not be in sync with how we want to treat our clients or make decisions."

Step 4. Accountability

Step 4 involves accountability and the metrics you need to see what kind of progress you're making in bringing the aspirational culture to life.

There are multiple ways you can tackle measurement, depending on where you are starting from and where you are trying to go. First, you could measure the extent to which different aspects of the aspirational culture are being demonstrated by people. You could ask for feedback on each of the values and/or on the behaviours that are associated with those values that you outlined in Step 2 and then measure how well those values are coming to life and where improvements are needed. Those types of measurement could be incorporated into an employee survey.

Another measurement approach is to determine if you're making progress against how embedded the culture is. For example, is the aspirational culture part of the language employees use with each other? Part of debriefing at the end of a project? Part of what it takes to be promoted? Are managers and leaders consistently behaving in ways that are consistent with the culture you strive to have? Find ways to solicit a range of perspectives on whether that's happening, perhaps through 360 feedback or as part of performance management and development.

Once you have built measurement approaches, you can start to think about the culture analytics and reporting approaches you might create. One of the most effective things I've seen is having culture one-pagers or culture scorecards to share at town halls or with board members at board meetings. A culture scorecard can have metrics related to the ability to attract candidates, attrition rates by key functions/departments and employee survey results that focus on overall perceptions of the culture and the extent to which each of the values are demonstrated by employees, managers and leaders. It can also track how many people have been onboarded or received other education related to the culture.

I have also created measures that combine these kinds of metrics into an overall, more comprehensive "culture score". This scorecard can also include quotes and stories from candidates and employees about the culture. Analytics that measure different aspects of the aspirational culture and that track progress over time send a message that culture is important and that the organisation is committed to making progress.

The last part of this is accountability. The reason why you're putting all this effort into culture is because you want to improve. You want to make the culture better. It's critical that there is clear accountability for whomever is responsible for culture improvements throughout an organisation. Optimally, this would be the CEO or a small team of senior leaders. It's their job to make sure everyone follows through to create an aspirational culture that is brought to life. I have seen some CEOs take this very seriously, explaining to employees that culture is one of the core responsibilities of their roles.

The consequences of not being intentional

This chapter started with a great example of how Leader Bank learned to be intentional about culture. Here's an example of what happened to an organisation that was not.

In 2019, Salesforce acquired Tableau in a significant $15.7bn deal to bolster its position in the analytics and data visualisation market. But from a people and culture perspective, this acquisition hasn't gone well. In fact, a large group of Tableau employees got together to have a wake for Tableau's culture – mourning the loss of a culture they loved. They made the press with the headline "'Tableau has been killed by Salesforce: Past and current Tableau employees gather at 'Irish wake'".[1] I had the opportunity to talk to some of these people, and they told me how disappointed they were with how culture was handled as Salesforce acquired them.

When the acquisition began, there appeared to be

alignment between Salesforce and Tableau's values. However, before long, the cracks started to show. For example, the shared understanding of the concept of trust, deemed by both companies as culturally important, differed significantly. Salesforce focused on customer trust, implementing strict internal controls on data and reporting. Tableau employees felt that Salesforce prioritised external trust over trust among colleagues, leading to restricted access to data and lots of formal process and approvals. These processes and approvals meant that they felt a lack of trust, and on top of that what they deemed unnecessary hassle and bureaucracy.

The lack of meaningful human connection between Tableau and Salesforce employees exacerbated the cultural challenges. The acquisition process, despite being well orchestrated with celebrations, lacked authenticity and genuine connection. Tableau employees wanted open communication and a chance for their voices to be heard, but they felt the focus was on corporate messaging and processes rather than building personal relationships. Human-to-human and culture-to-culture interactions were lacking throughout the acquisition.

Another cultural hurdle stemmed from the divergent priorities of the two companies. Salesforce prioritised sales, whereas Tableau placed greater value on product quality and customer impact. The culture of Salesforce came across as shallow, excessively positive and lacking substance to Tableau employees, who sought more meaning and depth. This misalignment of core values contributed to the challenges faced during the integration process.

Ultimately, the lack of shared understanding and a failure to intentionally address cultural differences led to employee departures and dissatisfaction among those who remained (with a likely impact on Tableau customers too). In early 2023, many former Tableau employees were laid off, including many senior leaders. Ironically, later that year Salesforce held a campaign to re-hire them.

Without a more intentional approach to culture as part of the acquisition, Salesforce ended up alienating the very people they needed to make the merger a success.

Remember

1. The first step of being intentional about culture is to create a shared vision of what the culture needs to be if the business is to succeed.

2. Everyone needs to understand the behaviours that are required. Values in action set clear behavioural expectations for everyone.

3. An ongoing commitment to culture education ensures that new and current employees are learning why culture matters and what it means for them.

4. Accountability and metrics are critical to ensure that progress is being made.

These first steps of the Intentional Culture Circle set the intention and direction for culture evolution. Next comes the hard work of bringing the culture to life.

6

Bringing culture to life

Simha Sadavisa, the CEO and co-founder of software company Ushur, comes from a modest background in India. His parents always focused on education and wanted to make sure he and his sister had a decent shot at upward mobility. After Simha graduated from college, he went on a plane for the first time when he was 23 years old to start his first job in the United States. He and his new wife had four suitcases, $400 and lots of ambition. Starting in Chicago and then moving to Silicon Valley, Simha and a friend and colleague, Henry Peter, decided to start Ushur.

Around the time that Simha and his wife moved to Silicon Valley, his parents came to live with them. Sadly, his mother was soon diagnosed with a terminal illness. Simha and the rest of his family found themselves dealing with multiple insurance companies and a complex and frustrating healthcare system.

That's where the idea of Ushur came from. Simha thought that the insurance process could be so much better, and that technology could help. As he puts it: "Why don't we try to "usher" people through these difficult journeys? We memorialised our intent with our company name by calling it Ushur."

Ushur has a leadership team that understands the importance of doing culture work and embedding it into everything they do. It started as a values-driven organisation (at least partially due to Simha and Henry being values-driven founders), understanding that people are their business. Over time, they articulated their values and, more recently, have behaviouralised them – that is, they have described their values in behavioural terms so that anyone who reads them understands what they look like in action. Now they are working to build their values more intentionally into everything they do.

As Simha said: "We know that in order to achieve scale, we have to have repeatability. This intentional repeatability will bring focus and efficiency to any business. And we know that is true for scaling our culture." When your organisation is small, it's relatively easy to make sure everyone is on the same page and shares the same set of values. But once you start to grow, especially with more people working remotely, it's harder to ensure that alignment and offer people a consistent cultural experience.

That's where the second section of the Intentional Culture Circle comes into play. Once you have defined the culture you need and everyone understands it, how do you make it real and repeatable? Not putting the effort and intention into making the culture come to life is one of the biggest mistakes I see in organisations when it comes to culture. Even the best aspirational culture needs to be woven into everything that happens on the ground.

As Harvard Business School professor Michael Beer said: "Culture gets changed by doing real work in line with the new strategy, a new governance model, business processes or performance management systems."[1] This is the real culture work. It's definitely not about shiny presentation decks and taglines. It's about making significant changes to the deeply entrenched ways in which an organisation works.

Figure 7b: **Intentional Culture Circle**

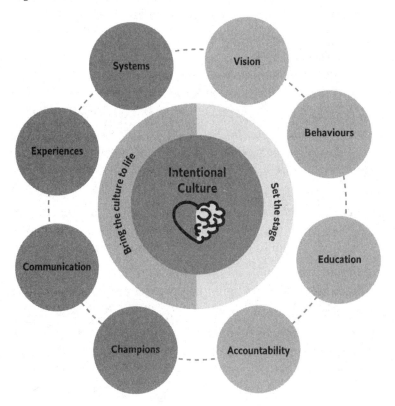

To avoid the negative outcomes of cultural betrayal – what happens when there is a mismatch between aspirational and experienced culture – you need to bring your culture to life. That means that the aspirational culture must bring together all the different practices, systems and other experience of the organisation. It's what makes consistent both the big experiences that employees might have (like being onboarded, going to their first all-hands meeting, being promoted) and the smaller experiences in their day-to-day work (like how their colleagues and manager treats them, the use of technology in their work, the attitude to taking breaks and having fun during the workday). It's a unifying and simple focus on what matters in your organisation.

This approach makes life in the organisation simpler, more straightforward, more unified, more aligned. Clear.

But what really happens in many organisations is that they aren't clear or unified. They look for all kinds of shiny objects – new leadership models, cool concepts that have flashy catchphrases and new corporate flavours of the day that are met with employee eye rolls. Or it's a new outside speaker or fun activity they can use at the next big all-hands meeting or incorporating a new hiring tool or software platform. Surely one of these will be the magic bullet, the answer to their problems?

In reality, these end up being distractions. Of course, there are always things you can learn from these shiny objects. But they can also sidetrack and distract you from the core task of what is, in essence, a simple, basic idea: how to bring people together and make a more aligned culture come to life.

Let's keep going around the culture circle, starting with the importance of culture champions.

Step 5. Champions

Culture champions – formal and informal – help embed culture on a daily basis and encourage people to see that culture is not just a mandate from above.

Having champions in organisational change work is important because they play a critical role in promoting and sustaining the culture effort over time. Champions are passionate about the change and are willing to take an active role in promoting and advocating for it.

You can find these champions in formal and informal ways. In many organisations, those people who are always involved, speaking up and asking questions can be great culture champions. However, using more democratic processes for identifying culture champions can create more of a sense of fairness about who is involved. You might even think about creating clear criteria and job descriptions, invite people to self-nominate and then have an impartial panel select the best candidates.

One organisation had each division select a representative who participated in a monthly conversation with the leadership team to talk about culture. Each of these monthly meetings had a specific topic and the culture representatives were encouraged to bring their ideas and feedback to the conversation. They were especially encouraged to bring hard news to this team. The leaders had set the stage to create psychological safety with these culture champions and continued to reinforce that throughout their time together. The conversations offered the leadership team an opportunity to learn what was happening on the ground in their organisation, develop meaningful relationships with employees they might not have met otherwise, and have people in each division who could share with other employees how much the organisation was committed to culture.

Research has shown that champions can have a significant impact on the success of organisational change initiatives. Champions act as change agents who help bridge the gap between leadership and employees, ensuring that cultural values and goals are effectively communicated and understood throughout the organisation.[2] Culture champions also serve as role models, embodying desired cultural behaviours and norms and inspiring and motivating others to embrace the change.[3]

Champions can create a sense of ownership and accountability, encouraging everyone to actively participate in the culture change process.[4] They can help sustain change efforts by embedding the new cultural values into day-to-day operations and influencing others to maintain and reinforce the aspirational behaviours.[5] Culture champions can also provide valuable feedback and insights and help to identify potential roadblocks and opportunities for improvement.

Champions should authentically believe in the culture work. It's good to have a mix of people from the perspectives of tenure in the company, location, gender, race, department and age, as well as other important demographics specific to your organisation.

Involve culture champions early and often – and make sure the work they do is recognised. Culture champions should have these responsibilities called out as part of their job, and their other work should be adjusted to make space for these important responsibilities.

When people hear how important culture is through the voice of champions, it can go so much further and have much more impact than hearing about culture through just a leader's voice.

Step 6. Communication

Communication is fundamental. It's important to take regular opportunities to connect the dots and to reinforce and encourage people who are demonstrating the new culture. When people are not clear about their organisation's culture, they may have different interpretations of what is acceptable behaviour, leading to confusion and conflict. Clear and continuing communication of the aspirational culture is essential for aligning behaviours and reinforcing how important culture is to the achievement of the organisation's goals.

When organisations communicate their aspirational culture regularly, it creates a sense of shared purpose and identity. Internal research at Facebook found that when people feel a sense of belonging and connection to their organisation, they are more engaged, committed and productive.[6]

Communication about aspirational culture is also crucial for attracting talent. According to research by Glassdoor, an online platform that provides insights on jobs and companies, over 77% of job seekers consider company culture before applying for a job, and 56% of employees would turn down a job offer if the culture did not meet their expectations.[7] This clear culture communication allows organisations to attract candidates who share those same values.

And when employees feel their organisation's culture aligns with their personal values, they are more likely to stay with the organisation in the long term. People also need regular communication about the culture to be able to understand if there is alignment with their own values.[8]

Think of this continuing focus on culture in terms of a regular drumbeat of communication that has a special rhythm and style of its own. Some of the best ways I've seen organisations develop this regular drumbeat is by having simple icons and pictures that represent the values and then using those regularly in meetings or as a first or last page in their company presentation deck templates. Another example is to share examples of employees demonstrating the culture formally and informally – for example, short videos that employees send in about how they see a colleague living one of the values. One company uses a slogan of "caught in the act" and showcases an employee who was demonstrating one of their values in action. The idea here is to be consistent in what you are saying about the culture in the messaging, how you say it and describe it, and finally how often you do that, which is way more often than it seems that you should.

If culture communication starts to feel like too much to the communicator, you probably still need to do a little more.

Step 7. Experiences

Visible demonstrations of culture are often how employees experience culture – at big meetings or at company celebrations. In many organisations, however, all the parts of the Intentional Culture Circle that come before this step are skipped. So, when culture is discussed at these kinds of meetings and parties, it is usually met with employee scepticism or at least a smirk. But if you have done the important work up to this point in this cycle, these meetings and celebrations can become validating and inspirational.

What's challenging and powerful about culture experiences is that the best ones are customised to an organisation. They are relevant and meaningful to the people on the inside, but an outsider might think they are silly or might not get it at all.

Some of the experiences of the culture can come from the design of offsites days and company meetings where employees learn about the culture and its connection to business strategy and results. It's powerful, for example, when organisations bring in customers to talk about the impact employees have had on them and how those employees exemplify the culture. I have also seen ridiculously silly skits, karaoke and giant tricycle races that seem to land well in some organisations. In one organisation, the focus is on building more collaboration, so there are collaborative fun activities like cross-group Lego-building contests and team mural painting. What's special about these experiences is that they are explicitly tied to what the organisation values, what it is trying to achieve and how important it is that everyone is doing this together.

Other powerful culture experiences show up in everyday life. Leader Bank, for example, has created its own way of bringing people together to build culture with a specific focus on learning, which is fundamental to its culture. It's called the Leadership Out of Office Program (LOOP).

People are divided into cross-departmental teams and each team leader is the cohort teacher for each group. The leaders meet in advance to discuss a shared learning topic. Sometimes they solicit ideas from team members in advance; sometimes they decide to learn about something that is relevant to the business at the time.

These leaders discuss the lesson plan: the material they want to share, the key points they are going to cover, what they want everyone to learn. But they also make space for differentiation; each leader can build in specific activities or examples or approaches they want to take. The overarching idea is that they support learning and that this learning is important to Leader Bank's success.

Another example is Trader Joe's, a grocery store chain known for its unique and quirky culture, which is focused on creating a fun shopping experience for customers. Team members, known as crew members, wear Hawaiian shirts and are encouraged to engage with customers and share their enthusiasm for their products. They are taught to care about the customer, not just to sell them something. They have seven golden rules that describe how they want team members to be with each other and with customers, including ideas like being part of the neighbourhood, integrity in how they operate and deal with customers, and an emphasis on teamwork and working together. Almost every one of the golden rules emphasises the importance of how team members treat each other and the customer.[9]

The phrase "taught to care" is what I mean by being intentional about culture. Make it crystal clear to employees what really matters.

Step 8. Systems

The alignment of systems, processes and practices is a huge component of being intentional about your culture.

Weaving the aspirational culture into systems and processes like hiring, onboarding, performance management and learning and development are obvious ways that the culture can feel real to employees. People practices and systems are the most obvious experience of culture. If the team that cares the most about people and culture is not aligned, how can we expect any other teams to be aligned and supportive of the aspirational culture?

People systems are, of course, just one of many systems in the organisation that can help (or hinder) the culture come to life. Financial systems, customer service protocols and vendor/ supplier contracts are other examples of how employees come to learn about what's really valued. But people practices are a great place to start to ensure that culture is truly experienced by employees.

Many organisations tend to think only about onboarding when they think about culture building. But there are many more opportunities to make the culture come to life, by embedding the aspirational culture into various aspects of the organisation.

Hiring

Use the aspirational culture in job advertisements and job descriptions. Develop legally defensible hiring criteria based on the behaviouralised values and selection processes that offer a realistic job preview of what the culture is like. Have honest and authentic conversations about the current and aspirational culture throughout the hiring process. Some organisations have filmed videos that describe the culture in a "day in the life" format, uncovering what's positive about the culture but also being realistic about the challenges and post those on their websites for candidates to view.

Onboarding

Develop standardised approaches to onboarding that educate new employees about the culture and the role they each play in bringing the culture to life. Culture should be a significant part of onboarding – this is one of the best times to educate new employees about the culture you are trying to create.

Performance management

Use a simple "what and how" model of performance that incorporates how people accomplish their work as much as the results they achieve. That is, make it clear that performance is broader than just the outcomes or results that a person achieves – just as important is how they do their work. The expectations for "how" can be articulated through behaviouralised values.

Learning and development

Connect learning and development at all levels with explicit values. Instead of searching for the latest development fad or shiny model, teach everyone about the aspirational culture and what that looks like behaviourally.

Job and organisational design

The division of labour, how jobs are designed and reporting relationships all send a message about what's valued in the organisation. Many organisations rely on traditional approaches to which roles they have and how they organise the roles and functions (eg, we have account managers because everyone in our industry has account managers) without being clear what they are prioritising (or not prioritising) in their culture by including them.

Benefits

Different from compensation and other rewards (see below), the benefits the organisation chooses to offer its employees and how the benefits are offered to employees also need to be aligned with the aspirational culture. For example, the outdoor clothing company Patagonia is very intentional about its culture and emphasises social and environmental responsibility. It provides employees with paid time off for environmental activism and sponsors numerous environmental initiatives.

Promotions

Promotion processes, career paths and career development activities need to be aligned with the aspirational culture. Which employees are promoted speaks volumes about what matters.

Employee handbook

The employee handbook is often one of the first formal and documented ways in which employees see what's important to an organisation. The content and the design should reflect the aspirational culture. If it doesn't, this is one of the first ways to create a disconnect between what someone was "sold" during the hiring process and what they actually "bought", now that they are an employee.

Termination/offboarding/alumni network

Who is asked to leave and how people leave also need to be aligned with your aspirational culture. Once people leave an organisation, how they were treated influences how they represent and talk about your company. There are many advantages in continuing to have a relationship with previous employees. Some companies have even established networks of former employees.

Beyond the people system, some of the other practices and systems that need to be aligned with the culture include the following.

Customer service/support approaches and protocols

Make sure that people who interface with your customers are educated and empowered to make decisions that are aligned with your culture. For example, if one of your values is to prioritise the needs of customers, make sure that the people who are interacting with customers have the authority and ability to help customers, and that they don't have to escalate routine issues or go through unnecessary bureaucracy.

Budgeting and expense and reimbursement policies

What gets funded and reimbursed, and what doesn't, sends a clear message to employees about what matters. For example, if growth and learning are part of your organisation's values, but learning opportunities are not reimbursed, employees may not feel that this value is authentically supported.

Strategic planning and funding of strategic initiatives

Which projects get selected and which don't and the amount of funding that strategic initiatives receive should be aligned with your culture. For example, if one of your values is related to innovation, strategic initiatives that support innovation should be prioritised and funded. Similarly, which objectives and key results (or other organisational goals) are chosen needs to be aligned with your values.

Vendor selection and contracting

How vendors are selected, which work is outsourced to vendors and how vendors are paid are opportunities for values alignment. Take, for example, an organisation that says it values diversity and inclusion. This organisation should have practices in place to encourage vendors from underrepresented communities to participate in their vendor selection process. Or take an organisation that provides software to small businesses and has values related to supporting them. It would be important for this organisation not to have vendor policies in place that go against this, such as taking a long time to pay their vendors or requiring high levels of business insurance.

Marketing and external communication

What is emphasised in how products and services are marketed and how the organisation is represented externally must align with what is valued internally. In some organisations there can be a real disconnect between external advertisements or communications and what they are emphasising culturally.

Scorecards and board reports

These measures of progress send a visible sign of what's valued. Make sure there is consistency and that your values are reflected in them. As mentioned earlier, incorporate the focus on your "aspire to" culture by including culture metrics in board reports. Unfortunately, I often see an internal focus on culture from the CEO with employees, but a hesitancy to share that focus more widely. This incongruity sends a message that the CEO is simply playing to the internal audience, not truly embracing the importance of culture.

Rewards and recognition

One of the most important systems in an organisation is the reward and recognition system; what gets rewarded is what gets repeated. To be intentional about culture means that you need to reward and reinforce employees (at all levels) who have demonstrated the culture. It also means that you need to deal with – even fire – people (at all levels) who actively work against the culture you're looking to achieve.

One of the most obvious ways to reward and recognise employees is through compensation. Decisions about how people are compensated should be connected to the approach to performance management described above, ensuring that those who are living the values and completing the tasks of the role are recognised through the compensation system at higher levels than those who are not demonstrating both the "what" and "how".

Before 2013, Microsoft's compensation and forced ranking system, known as "stack ranking", was a system in which managers were required to rate employees on a curve with a fixed percentage of employees receiving high scores, a fixed percentage receiving low scores, and the remaining employees receiving scores in between. The system was designed to create competition among employees and to identify and reward top performers, as well as to weed out poor performers. However, it had many negative outcomes.

The system fostered internal competition and created norms of backstabbing and politicking among employees, as they competed for higher rankings and tried to avoid being ranked at the bottom. This competition and individualism often came at the expense of collaboration and teamwork. There was also a disconnect between this focus on competition and what the company was trying to achieve at the time: the development of collaboration software.

The system was also seen as unfair, as it relied heavily on subjective evaluations by managers. This led to a sense of disillusionment among people who felt that their hard work and contributions were not being recognised or rewarded.

It was ineffective in identifying and retaining top talent, as it often resulted in the loss of high performers who were ranked at the bottom because of the fixed percentage system. As a result, this system created a revolving door of people, as those who were ranked at the bottom were often fired or forced to resign, leading to high turnover rates and a loss of institutional knowledge and expertise.

The performance management and associated

compensation system had a large negative impact on Microsoft's culture, which will take years to turn around. So, starting in 2013, Microsoft embarked on a departure from its traditional approach. It introduced a new system known as One Microsoft which aimed to create a more inclusive, collaborative and innovative work culture. To achieve this, Microsoft bid farewell to the previous stack ranking system and instead embraced a more progressive approach centred around continuous feedback and development. The focus shifted from an annual review cycle to fostering regular conversations and support between managers and team members.

Microsoft's decision to change its performance review process has had mixed results. On the positive side, people report feeling more supported and empowered, with increased opportunities for growth and development. The new system also led to the elimination of forced rankings, which were seen as demoralising. However, some critics argue that the changes have created a more lenient and less accountable environment, with concerns raised about potential biases in evaluating performance. Some Microsoft employees I have talked to appreciate the efforts to evolve the performance review process but are concerned that there is now a less transparent process for determining their review scores, with a process similar to stack ranking happening behind the scenes.

Overall, the impact of Microsoft's performance review process changes has been a complex mix of benefits and challenges, reflecting the complexities of transforming the culture of a large organisation. What is clear is the link between systems and culture, especially the rewards and recognition system. Who and what is rewarded is an important indicator of what is really valued.

Recognising those who are living the values

Aligning reward and recognition programmes to a company's values and culture is a surefire way to be clear about the importance you place on them.

Marriott International has a programme called Spirit to Serve, which recognises people who exemplify the company's values. Employees who are recognised receive a certificate, a pin, and are entered into a draw for a trip for two to any Marriott property in the world. Similarly, Samsung, the South Korean multinational conglomerate, has a programme called the Global Samsung Awards, which recognises employees who demonstrate the company's core values. Winners receive a monetary prize, a trophy and a certificate of achievement.

In one company I worked at, twice a year we recognised people for demonstrating each of our values. Those who were selected were recognised in front of the company and how they demonstrated the values was described in detail by someone who knew the recipient well. The award was a small, symbolic award made by an artist engraved with their names and the value they demonstrated. These values awards seemed to be truly meaningful to the employees.

These more formal programmes go a long way to create clarity about the importance of organisational values. But more informal recognition can be even more powerful. Empowering peers and managers to reinforce other employees who are demonstrating the aspirational culture can often have more of a reinforcing effect than more formal programmes. This can be accomplished through recognition programmes that have the values integrated into them, so that day-to-day examples of living the values can be recognised. This kind of informal recognition can be implemented using technology platforms but also more informally. One company simply offered employees notecards with the logos for each of the values on them so they could write a simple note of recognition to one of their colleagues.

Just as important as recognising those who demonstrate the values, however, is the opposite. If people are actively working against the aspirational culture, they need to be dealt with. First, you need to be sure that they understand your behavioural expectations (outlined in Step 2). Then you need to help them work through any barriers they have in understanding and performing them.

If someone is still not willing to live up to the behavioural expectations, more serious changes need to be made. Ultimately, they should be asked to leave the organisation and find another organisation more in line with what they value and how they behave. It's important, of course, to be fair and clear but also to act. And as the amount of power the employee in question has increases, the more important this is dealt with in a timely manner.

The most infamous example of such a lack of action is probably the case of Enron, the US energy company. Enron had listed "integrity" in its corporate values statement. Yet in 2001 the company was involved in one of the biggest corporate scandals in history, when it was revealed that the company had engaged in fraudulent accounting practices. Enron will forever be known as the poster child for a misaligned culture.

In 2019, Nike was accused of fostering a toxic work culture that included harassment and discrimination against female employees. The athletic clothing company's values include "diversity and inclusion" and "ethics and compliance". Nike faced criticism for not doing enough to address the allegations and for rewarding executives who had been accused of misconduct. Similarly, Kobe Steel, the Japanese steel and engineering company, had a value of "quality first" in its corporate values statement. However, the company was involved in a scandal in 2017 when it was discovered that it had falsified data on the quality of its products.

Simply having company values listed on a website does not guarantee that they will be demonstrated on the ground. The work that is described throughout the Intentional Culture Circle is what makes your culture come to life.

The challenge of culture complexity

Woven Planet, a subsidiary of the automotive company Toyota, faced a particularly tricky cultural challenge: how to integrate a Silicon Valley culture with Toyota's distinct Japanese values. The purpose of this new company, founded in 2021, was to take the best of both of those cultures and bring them together to help Toyota create software innovation for all its cars.

Toyota is the largest employer in Japan and almost 100 years old. Much of the culture that has made Toyota successful is also very similar to Japanese culture more widely. And, of course, Silicon Valley is known for creating market-changing (and life-changing) innovation. These geographical locations both have tangible cultures that have been translated into business or industry outcomes.

Toyota is also known for its excellence at large-scale manufacturing, reproducing high quality in mass quantities on a global scale in a very cost-efficient way. But the nature of that excellence, reproducing the same item at volume, can run counter to innovation – what Silicon Valley is known for. How could the new company create a new culture from a combination of the best of both worlds? And effectively combine these cultures to deliver software at scale to Toyota?

The cultural complexity involved was immense. As Carrie

Olesen, the Chief People Officer at Woven Planet, reflects: "How do you create a generic enough technology platform that everyone can participate in and that will scale and be global? Thinking at scale, thinking globally, thinking collaboratively?" In addition, there's the struggle of balancing the need to make long-term decisions about hardware design (decisions that are made years ahead of time) with the fast-paced, constant innovation of software. These product and business complexities are added on to the natural tensions between the two cultures. Carrie knew that they had to be thoughtful about the culture and behaviours they need to succeed.

The companies started by being specific about how they wanted to work together. And they always connected it back to "why" – the specific aspects of their strategy that required their aspirational culture to be demonstrated by everyone, even though there wasn't always a shared understanding.

Although Woven Planet is still in the middle of this work, it has already done a lot to be intentional about culture. Some early steps included being thoughtful about which leaders were chosen to run different parts of the company and how power and authority are given – working to move it deeper into the organisation, not just keeping it at the top.

Woven Planet is also aligning its work to The Toyota Way, a set of principles that defines the organisational culture and Toyota Production System, including embedding its software production process into that existing framework. This provides a common working framework, and an acknowledgement of what Toyota has been doing so well.

In addition to aligning with the production framework, Carrie also made sure that the people system was aligned – creating behavioural expectations and ensuring that onboarding, performance management and promotions were all aligned to the culture they aspire to.

Woven Planet also measured employee attitudes and perceptions of how things are going, and it is also measuring the impact on customers, making sure that the way customers experience the company is landing in a culturally aligned way. The alignment between the culture and the mission and purpose of Woven Planet is critical – and making culture come to life throughout the business creates a virtuous cycle of cultural reinforcement.

Culture work is never-ending

The cyclical nature depicted in the Intentional Culture Circle is important; it represents a process that never ends. As your organisation's environment changes and your business strategy evolves with it, culture needs to transform to reflect these changes. Think about culture work as an evolution that, like anything else that is challenging and important, never really ends.

That said, the first time around the circle will probably be the most challenging one. After that, everyone will expect that there will be work on the culture. Although it is never-ending, it won't always feel overwhelming.

Making progress: culture change maturity model

In Chapter 2, I talked about the different categories of articulation and experience of the culture: cultural voids, leadership opportunities, cultural betrayal and intentional culture. Once your organisation is on the intentional culture journey, there still are many different stages that an organisation can go through to become more and more intentional.

Getting to the point of being intentional about culture is a

Figure 8: **Culture maturity model**

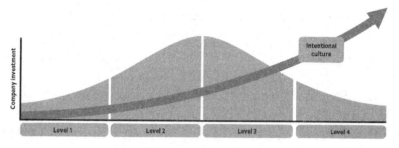

big step. Then you can use the culture maturity model to find where your organisation is now (see Figure 8), where you can go next, and what you can aspire to.

Level 1. Surface-level culture

At the first level of culture maturity, the organisation possesses values that are present but remain merely words displayed on walls or websites. Although these values exist, they are not deeply ingrained or actively practised throughout the company. Culture work is perceived as peripheral, as a nice-to-have, rather than being strategically linked to the overall success of the organisation.

In this stage, culture committees are assigned the responsibility for cultivating the culture, often resulting in activities such as parties and distributing company swag. Leaders tend to delegate the culture work to these committees, and may lack active involvement or commitment themselves. This level reflects a limited understanding of the profound impact that culture can have on the company's performance and the need for a more strategic approach to shaping and embedding desired cultural behaviours.

Level 2. Developing culture

At the second level of culture maturity, the organisation moves beyond having values as mere words and begins to develop a deeper understanding of what those values look like in action. Detailed descriptions of how the values manifest in day-to-day behaviours are created, providing employees with a clear sense of expectations. Values are communicated to employees through company meetings, ensuring that they are aware of and aligned with the organisation's cultural aspirations.

Additionally, the values are integrated into certain aspects of the people system, such as the hiring process, ensuring that cultural alignment is considered when bringing new talent on board. At this level, the HR leader takes the lead in driving culture work, and other leaders may not view themselves as directly accountable for shaping the culture. Because of that, the culture is not likely to be experienced in other ways – like the financial and operational aspects of the business. However, the organisation is making progress by actively defining and communicating its values and incorporating them into key areas of the employee experience.

Level 3. Consistent culture

At the third level of culture maturity, values are not just discussed sporadically but are consistently present throughout the organisation. The recognition of the impact of culture on business results becomes more apparent, and the connection between culture and organisational success is acknowledged and actively promoted. Leaders begin to see themselves as culture leaders, understanding the crucial role they play in shaping and modelling the desired culture. However, not all leaders may be held fully accountable for demonstrating the culture at this stage.

The values are woven into various aspects of the people system, including hiring processes, onboarding programmes, performance management systems and employee development initiatives. The organisation demonstrates a more comprehensive and integrated approach to embedding the culture throughout the employee lifecycle, recognising that cultural alignment is vital for individual and organisational effectiveness. At this level, the culture is also experienced consistently outside of the people system, including operationally and externally.

Level 4. Embedded culture

The fourth and final level of culture maturity represents an organisation that is fully committed to the work of culture and embraces it as an integral part of its identity. At this level, the organisation demonstrates agility by adapting the values and culture to changes in the environment and strategic shifts. All leaders, without exception, see themselves as culture leaders and actively embody the desired cultural behaviours.

Values become deeply ingrained in the language of the organisation and are seamlessly woven into every facet of the organisation's systems. All employees, including leaders, are held accountable for being culture role models, reinforcing the values through their actions and decisions. The desired culture becomes so ingrained and natural that it defines who the organisation is and shapes everything it does. The "aspire to" culture aligns with the experiences of employees, creating a harmonious and authentic environment where the desired culture is reflected in every aspect of the organisation's operations.

Moving to this level of culture maturity takes time, but having a realistic understanding of where you are now helps you set expectations for what progress looks like as you become more intentional about culture.

Remember

1. Champions and communications are the beginning of bringing your culture to life. Making sure there is a regular drumbeat about the culture from all levels of the organisation is one way to make it real.

2. Customised, authentic experiences of the culture create opportunities for employees to come together and create real connections through the culture.

3. Make sure that practices and systems, especially (but not only) those related to the people system, are all aligned to the aspirational culture. This is an opportunity to create a more unified and aligned workforce.

4. Finally, culture work is never-ending and each organisation should continue to strive to be more intentional.

So far, throughout this book, I have indicated how important power and leaders are to understanding and transforming culture. In the next chapter, I will dig into why that is true, and look at different types of organisational power and how we can all use our power to help improve culture.

7

Culture and power

In 2015, Volkswagen was charged with unlawfully installing software to cheat required emissions tests. The company was fined over $20bn in what is considered the biggest automotive scandal in the world to date. On the surface this just seems as if Volkswagen responded to a technical problem with a technical answer, albeit unethically: its cars couldn't pass rigorous US emissions requirements and Volkswagen was trying desperately to compete in the US market. But dig deeper into what was happening inside Volkswagen and you can see how power and culture influenced this outcome.

Aggressive sales and market share targets had been set and leaders were putting immense pressure on people to reach them. This pressure led to extreme competition and a climate of fear. And because of this fear, employees did not voice dissenting opinions or challenge unethical ideas about how to address the emissions issues.

Instead, they reported being afraid of the consequences for their jobs and careers, or of being excluded from the company's bonus programme, if they blew the whistle on this unethical behaviour. It was clear to everyone the priority was the short-term sales goals, not ethical behaviour.[1]

The leadership pressure that created this fear meant that unethical shortcuts to meet those goals were not confronted.

And that led directly to the scandal. There is a clear connection here between power, culture and scandal.

There's a reason this book is called *The Power of Culture*. Power and culture are inextricably linked: to understand culture, you need to understand how it relates to power. Culture and organisational power go hand in hand.

What is organisational power?

Organisational power is the influence that individuals or groups at work have to make decisions, control resources and shape the behaviour and actions of others. Those with organisational power can have an impact on outcomes, guide the direction of the organisation and exercise authority.

Social psychologists John French and Bertram Raven have shown us that power shows up in organisations in multiple ways.[2]

First is what most of us think about when we think about power: **positional power**. This kind of power is about a person's formal role or level in the organisation, like a CEO or CFO.

Expert power is another kind of power that is about having special knowledge or expertise.

Referent power is the kind of power that is based on having positive relationships and connection with others. Typically, people with referent power are respected and admired, and often have charisma.

People with **informational power** have access and control to information and resources.

Reward power is having power over how rewards, resources and recognition are doled out.

And finally, the type of organisational power that involves punishment or other negative consequences is called **coercive power**.

Each of these kinds of power can uniquely influence specific aspects of culture. For example, referent power, based on admiration and respect, can foster a culture of collaboration, trust and strong interpersonal relationships. People who possess referent power can serve as role models, influencing the overall cultural norms and values. Informational power, stemming from access to valuable information, can shape a culture that values transparency, open communication and data-driven decision-making. Coercive power, based on fear or punishment, can create a culture of compliance and limited autonomy, stifling creativity and engagement. Those with expert power, stemming from knowledge and skills, can contribute to a culture that values expertise and continuous learning. People with expert power can inspire a culture of innovation and excellence.

As you were reading through these types of power, you might have been thinking about people who have multiple types of power. Many people do. And power is compounding: when a person has multiple types of power, they have more power overall.

Think about how power plays out in your organisation. Who makes the decisions? Who decides what the agenda is for big meetings? Who influences which annual goals are set? And when things get tough, who is the "go to" person or team that is asked to pull the organisation through? Understanding the power dynamics in your organisation can help you better understand how things get done and how you can be more effective.

Power is not necessarily bad

Power isn't necessarily a bad thing. Of course, power can corrupt, and it does. It can feel controlling and punitive. But power can also be used to inspire and unite people. Have you ever been in a group of people that is leader-less when you are trying to achieve a goal? Something simple like deciding where to go for dinner can quickly become frustrating. Having one person step up and use their informational or referent power to bring everyone together to make the decision and create a plan can be a relief.

Organisational challenges are likely to require much more clarity of direction and unification to bring everyone along. That's when power can be used to bring people together and encourage the mobilisation of collective creativity and focus. When needed, there has to be a decision-maker. As executive coach Kevin Williams told me: "Consensus all the time is irrational. There are times when consensus actually destroys value. We don't have time to take a roll call right now. Right? Like if your kid is walking in the street. Someone needs to see that and go snatch them out of the street." Someone needs to take the lead.

So, power is an important tool to help organise people and help them all come together to make progress – and to achieve results. There is nothing more powerful than a group of people working together with positivity and energy when culture is aligned. If you have ever been a part of a group that has this cultural connection and who work together very well, you know what that can feel like – it's truly powerful and inspiring.

Culture is powerful because it shapes behaviour

Culture is powerful because it shapes the behaviour of everyone in an organisation. It sends messages that help guide behaviour. And because humans learn and adapt and are typically motivated to fit in and keep their jobs, they typically become part of the culture.

Because culture is formed slowly, over time, through learning from others and from the environment, people look to those who have made it in the group as some of the primary people they learn from. Typically, it's inferred that people who are more senior and powerful in the organisation are those they should learn from. And through this process, they draw conclusions about what's important – through explicit, overt messages and behaviour, and implicit, subtle messages and behaviour from people in positions of power. Employees learn and modify their behaviour based on what those with power value.

Power is a mechanism for creating cultural conformity – which isn't necessarily good or bad. It is about all the nudges in the work environment that push people to conform. The underlying mechanism behind this behavioural nudging and reinforcement is based on how people in positions of power might reward or punish different behaviours. How people think about and react to power, how they value the perspective of those in positions of power, is also important. The desire to keep their jobs or get a pay rise or promotion or fit in might be enough motivation for this cultural conformity to occur.

Peer-based social influence (as opposed to the social influence of someone with positional power) might also lead to behavioural conformity, but the consequences of peer-based pressure to conform often has less of a long-term impact. Peer influence is unlikely to impact people's safety and security like keeping your job or getting a pay rise does.

Power and culture are intertwined

Some scholars even *define* culture in terms of power. For example, for educational researcher Richard Bates: "Culture is a complex mosaic of negotiation (and sometimes rebellion), constantly shaped by the exercise of various forms of power."[3] Defining culture by how power is exercised demonstrates the tight connection.

To complicate matters, *how* power is valued culturally indicates the extent to which power shapes culture. For example, in its simplest form, if the organisation is hierarchical, then positional power is likely to have more of an influence on the culture than if the organisation is not hierarchical.

Related to this is the idea of shared power. Within the organisational structure, how much power do leaders, managers and employees have? Does power tend to be decentralised so that many people within the organisation are able to make decisions and use their discretion? Or does power tend to be centralised to a very few people at the top or within certain functions (eg, the CEO and the CFO)? If a particular function (like marketing or product development) has more power because it is valued more than other functions, there are implications for what gets reinforced in the culture. So not only does power influence culture, but also culture influences perceptions of power.

This can vary from organisation to organisation. Take this cartoon (Figure 9) that was created to compare big technology companies.[4] The cartoonist depicts what matters in each organisation and shows who holds the power. For example, at Oracle, the legal function holds more power than engineering; at Microsoft, there is so much competition between big divisions that guns are used to represent the relationship. Of course, this is a cartoon. But it's a compelling way to think about

Figure 9: **Structure and power of major technology companies**

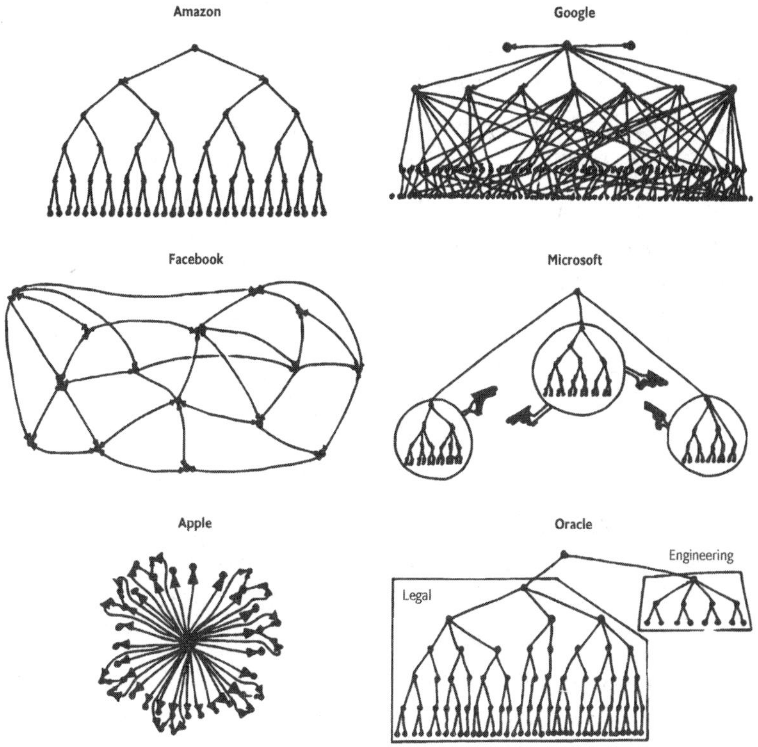

Amazon Google Facebook Microsoft Apple Oracle Engineering Legal

Source: Manu Cornet, bonkersworld.net

differences in organisational structure, power and culture.

Organisations have traditionally been structured in a hierarchical, leader-led way. But what about organisations that are not structured in this traditional manner?

A decentralised autonomous organisation (DAO) is an entity with no central leadership, where no one is assigned formal, positional power. Decisions are made from the bottom up, governed by a community organised around a specific set of rules. DAOs are owned and managed by their members. These are structures that are relatively new, mostly associated with organisations that exist primarily on the internet and have their own unique incentive models to get people to participate.

DAOs were developed to improve the traditional management structure, intending to give every member a voice to propose direction and initiatives. The idea was to move away from having a small group of leaders with the most power making all the decisions. That said, there are strict rules and governance models for how work gets done.[5]

But even in DAOs, leaders still emerge: people not with positional power, but instead with expert, informational, referent and sometimes coercive power. These leaders emerge through their ability to form clear arguments and influence others, and they do seem to have an influence on the culture of the DAO. Is this because we are so accustomed to traditional hierarchical models of how organisations are run that we can't help but fall back to what we know? Or is it because groups of people who work together need the clarity and direction that leadership (and power) can provide? Either way, leaders still emerge in structures that don't formally define them. And those leaders have an impact on the culture of the group.

The culture triangle

In one company I worked at, I attended an immersive development course called Power & Systems. During this six-day course based on a pretend society (where we lived in a pretend town), I was assigned a particular role as an immigrant. Some participants were elites, who owned and controlled much of the society's resources, and others were managers who needed to navigate between the immigrants and the elites. One of the biggest takeaways was that, in life as well as in manufactured immersive experiences, people often assume certain roles and mindsets based on the roles they are assigned. The same is true of culture at work. People with different roles typically play specific roles with culture too. These roles can work in harmony or they can create tension. And one of the biggest tensions I see related to roles and culture is when leaders take a stand about culture without involving managers in the work.

Managers caught in the middle

I often see managers identified as the "bad guys" or "bad gals", the reason employees are struggling or why people leave. If you have had a bad manager, you can understand this. But the often-repeated idea that people don't leave companies, they leave managers is oversimplified.

Managers are often the ones who are caught in the middle. They are the point where the aspirations from above meet the reality from below. And they are often caught in the tension of a culture triangle (see Figure 10); like the Bermuda Triangle, where the Gulf Stream winds intersect with the shallow water of the large number of islands in the Caribbean.

This confluence of aspiration and reality creates a lot of pressure for managers. They are expected to take the aspirations from above and translate and operationalise them to meet the realities of the day, often with no training, no support, little communication and few resources.

This can be thought of as a mini version of the cultural betrayal seen in Chapter 2. Managers often cannot deliver what people think was promised them. And so the psychological contract (the mutual beliefs, perceptions and informal obligations between an employer and an employee) that people have with the organisation is broken by the manager.[6] Hence, they blame the manager and not the organisation.

Figure 10: **The culture triangle**

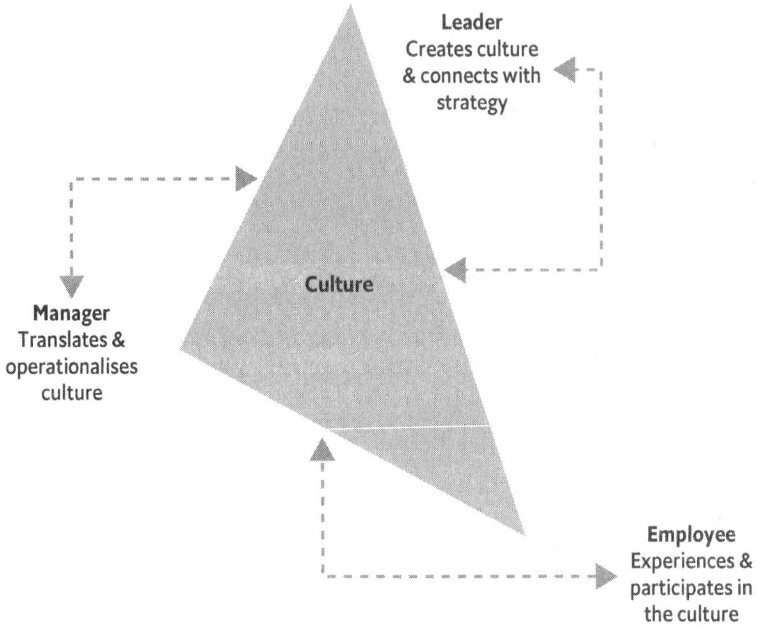

This is a problem. Instead, leaders must understand that they create the conditions for the culture to come to life. They must educate managers, support them and empower them to make day-to-day decisions that reinforce the culture. And employees aren't passive in this interaction either. How they respond and interact with other people in the organisation has an impact on the culture too.

Beliefs about your own power

How people think about their own power also affects their relationship with power more generally. If people believe they have a voice, that they matter and they have choices, they may challenge organisational values, norms and beliefs. While some employees might leave (and perhaps be a catalyst for change if they leave en masse), others may stay and help to influence the culture.

Some organisations have worked out how to use employee power to the benefit of their culture efforts. In others, employee power can be seen as a form of resistance that works against leadership efforts. The important thing to understand is that mandates from above to conform are typically not effective (at least not for the long run). Culture work is most effective when it harnesses the energy of everyone in an organisation.

The influence of where you live and work

Where you live and work also influences your relationship with power and how it might show up in your work cultures. "Power distance", a term coined by social psychologist Geert Hofstede, refers to the strength of a society's social hierarchy.[7] Power distance measures the extent to which people who are at the lower end of the hierarchy accept the fact that social stance or power is not distributed equally in that society. A culture that gives deference to a person of authority is a high-power distance culture. A culture that values the equal treatment of everyone is a low-power distance culture.

Think of how these differences in the national/geographical culture might influence organisational culture. For example, in Japan, indirect communication and reading between the lines are valued. This can lead to a more subtle and implicit communication style.[8] In Scandinavian countries, such as Sweden, work–life balance is a priority. Organisations in these cultures often promote flexible working hours, parental leave and a focus on employee well-being.[9] In Germany, there's a consensus-based decision-making culture known as *mittelstand*, where decisions are made through discussion and consultation among employees and managers. This contributes to a more collaborative and participatory organisational culture.[10]

Sometimes when I bring up the topic of power with my clients, there's an automatic negative response, a type of visceral rejection of elitism and hierarchy, which I get. But understanding how power dynamics work in your organisations and your environment is critical to creating cultures that value human beings. All systems with humans have power and power dynamics. You need to understand power and how it plays out in your organisation to create better cultures.

Positional power vs other types of power

At the beginning of this chapter, I outlined the different kinds of organisational power. Positional power, derived from formal authority, is what comes to mind when thinking about how power influences culture; that is, how leaders and others in the organisation with formal authority shape the culture. But it is important not to lose sight of the fact that other kinds of organisational power can also shape culture. Let's look at how different groups within organisations can do just that.

Leaders, power and culture

The role of leaders within an organisation is crucial in shaping its culture. An organisation's leaders should be role models for its culture, setting an example for others to follow. They need to understand the impact they have because of their position and perceived power. They need to make conscious efforts to create a positive and supportive work environment, and be aware of, and intentional about, the messages they are sending to others about what's important. The messages leaders convey about what is important greatly impact the organisation's values and priorities.

Leaders need to think of themselves as culture architects, taking accountability for the values and norms of the organisation and being intentional about how their actions and communications align with the culture they aspire to have.

Leaders also need to understand their power and how their values and beliefs may be different from what their employees value and from what the organisation needs to be successful. One of my observations after working with many different leaders is that leaders are often not aware of their power. This lack of awareness happens on two levels.

First, leaders fail to understand what kind of power they have and how they might use it – a real missed opportunity. For example, imagine a leader at an all-hands meeting who doesn't step in to help clarify when someone asks a question about the direction the company is headed and instead just leaves the question hanging. This could have been a great opportunity for the leader to embrace their power and help create clarity.

Second, leaders might also fail to understand how their actions might be misinterpreted. They often don't understand that all their actions, no matter how small, send a loud message about what's valued and what's not valued in the organisation. Leaders are like culture megaphones. Employees are looking for cues from them about what matters. For example, when a leader decides to leave early from a meeting where people are sharing their perspectives on an important issue. Or the leader checks their phone during a highly anticipated meeting. What did they smile or frown about? Did they interrupt someone? What joke did they tell? Was that ambiguous sentence a message about the future of that team? People can make mistaken assumptions about the meaning behind even the most innocent actions.

To give a real-life example, in one organisation a leader

was frustrated about an outcome that wasn't achieved and ended up yelling at a couple of people in a larger group. From his perspective, the message needed to be delivered and he thought he needed to demonstrate a sense of urgency. But this lack of awareness of his power was glaring. The message he was sending wasn't about accountability or urgency, but instead was that if you make a mistake you will get in big trouble, publicly. And the impact was real; not only were the recipients embarrassed but they were also scared.

Unfortunately, this leader's behaviour was also directly in conflict with the organisation's aspirational values. In one interaction, big messages were sent from the leader's actions to the organisation about what *really* mattered.

From my perspective, I completely understand why leaders want to take these kinds of actions. It's a hard and often frustrating job to lead an organisation. But that's why leaders get paid a lot of money – to handle that pressure, not to push that pressure on to other people. Instead, this leader could have asked questions and determined what needed to change in the organisation to get the results he was looking for and/or to make sure this same mistake didn't happen again.

Leaders must understand the importance of their roles as culture leaders. The culture can be strong enough to reject those who do not gel with it. Of course, if the culture is healthy, this rejection can be a good thing. But if it's not, and leaders who are trying to build new cultures get rejected, culture change will be stymied. The culture cycle (either virtuous or vicious) has the inertia to continue without significant intentional intervention.

Changing culture requires power. The tricky part is that, if the power is positional, the leaders who yield that power in organisations are part of the current system. Remember the example of how I started out in an organisation by collaborating and helping others, but then conformed to the values and norms? I stopped helping people and instead started looking out for myself. I became part of the system and could no longer even see it. Many leaders are long-term members of their organisational system and no longer see it for what it is. Often, these leaders were recruited and promoted for demonstrating the very behaviours that are part of the current culture. Not only is it hard for leaders to see their own behaviour but it's also extremely difficult for them to be motivated to change a system that has reinforced them psychologically and financially. And that doesn't include those leaders who lack self-awareness about their power or those who choose to use their power for their own interests.

A colleague gave the example of the CEO of her company (part of Fortune's Global 500) saying, during an executive staff meeting, that the employees should be 110% committed to the company. Someone mentioned that quite a few employees had second jobs or side hustles to help pay their bills, so it was hard to be that committed. He replied that nobody should be moonlighting. The room went quiet. The CEO acquiesced that "100% fully committed" would be the goal.

My colleague and her colleagues left that session feeling like the CEO was completely out of touch with what people were experiencing and that he was coming from a place of economic privilege. The one person who gave a different perspective was quickly shot down by the person with the most power in the room. The CEO left that conversation with his original misinformed perspective not only still in place but also reinforced: that he was primarily concerned with employee commitment to the company, not in understanding or empathising with what employees were going through.

It's only when leaders separate their own egos and interests and embrace the opportunity to use their power for good that they can create intentional cultures.

Many books about culture are focused on leadership for these reasons. Some leaders can step outside themselves and realise that change is needed. But if you rely on leaders as the only ones who decide the culture needs to change, you aren't going to make much progress. The more everyone can really understand culture and start working to change these systems, the better.

Leaders seek to maintain control and keep their power. Threats to a leader's power will often be met with a withdrawal or reduction of the power sharing with employees. Or there might be rounds of layoffs for organisations that are highly profitable – what a way to re-establish who is in charge. Organisations where grassroots movements have changed the culture successfully probably already had leaders who were open to using their power for good.

How can leaders be better culture drivers?

1. Embrace their roles as culture architects. Be the voice of the aspirational culture and work to design an intentional culture.

2. Understand their own power and how their behaviours impact others.

3. Study the current culture from the perspective of employees, understanding that their experience of the culture is likely to be different.

4. Hire other leaders who represent other perspectives than their own.

5. Learn about culture and specifically learn about how other types of culture like professional, national/ geographical and social identity cultures intersect with the organisation's culture.

6. Develop skillsets related to creating psychological safety.

7. Ensure the aspirational culture has human elements that include belonging, inclusion and caring about employees as human beings.

Founders

Founders, as the first leaders of an organisation, have a special impact on culture: they create or form it. When founders start a company, the culture either works (and then is shared by others as the company grows) or it doesn't (the company fails or is acquired, or a new leader is found).

The culture of most organisations can be linked to the personality characteristics of its founders. For example, "precision questioning" (asking repeated questions with increasing levels of specificity) has long been part of Microsoft's culture. Bill Gates, its founder, was well known for doing this. If a founder is more data-driven, the culture is likely to reflect that with more metrics and scorecards. If a founder is more focused on sales and marketing, the company is likely to prioritise that. Or if a founder is more contemplative and thoughtful, the culture may be slower to respond. These points reinforce the idea that power shapes culture. And that culture is enduring and deeply rooted.

Think about your own organisation. Do you know the founder or founders? Which aspects of your current culture might you be able to link back to their personalities, preferences or areas of expertise?

How can founders be better at forming culture?

1. Embrace their roles as culture architects early on (when they are the leaders of the organisation). Be the voice of the aspirational culture and work to design an intentional culture from the beginning.

2. Learn more about how their own personality and preferences influence the culture. Seek out other perspectives and points of view that should be represented in the founding values.

3. Be careful about connecting founding values to short-term goals. What's the bigger vision they have and what do they need everyone focusing on to meet that vision?

4. Don't be too quirky. Although in the moment, funny phrases and catchy slogans can feel right, if the organisation plans on sticking around, develop a culture vision and values that will age well.

5. Choose a board that fundamentally values culture.

Boards

In the Volkswagen example at the beginning of this chapter, the first domino to fall was the aggressive sales and market targets. Often, it is the boards who put this pressure on organisations to achieve ever higher results. And these boards are often disconnected from what it will take to achieve these goals. Boards should talk with leaders about the culture costs that come with aggressive or short-term goals. And they should be monitoring the culture overall, even to the point of providing culture governance. Unfortunately, most boards align with traditional board activities and only get tangentially involved with understanding and monitoring culture through executive compensation committees.

Many of the boards I have worked with have not held the CEO accountable for bringing them information about the culture. If they do ask about culture, they tend to take the CEO's word for it, rather than looking for data and evidence. Worse yet, many boards don't seem to understand what culture is, thinking anything that is people related is "culture". The lack of understanding about culture, the lack of stable governance and regular tracking, and the pressure from boards to achieve aggressive and short-term goals can often put pressure on the organisation that might not align with internal plans for being intentional about culture. Organisations that put strategic culture plans and metrics in front of boards have more of an opportunity to drive the culture conversation.

In the future (if it isn't already), culture is much more likely to be valued by your organisation's board. For example, the National Association of Corporate Directors (NACD) in the United States recommends: "The board, the CEO and senior management need to establish clarity on the foundational elements of values and culture – where consistent behaviour is expected across the entire organisation regardless of geography or operating unit – and develop concrete incentives, policies and controls to support the desired culture."[11] Companies need to start prioritising culture work because boards will start demanding it.

How can boards be better at culture governance?

1. Work with the organisation to develop strategic culture measures (eg, culture scorecards).
2. Include those measures in regular board meeting conversations about the state of the business.

3. Ask questions and ask for updates about culture; monitor and track progress.

4. Make sure leaders are culture role models and take action on those who are not.

5. Do not dismiss or sideline cultural issues as not relevant to the business. Culture is always relevant to business success.

6. Do not take only the CEO's word for what's happening with the culture. Dig deeper and look for evidence.

7. Ensure executive compensation performance criteria include culture measures.

Managers

If senior leaders and founders are the ones who form and transform culture, managers are the ones who ensure these norms, values and beliefs come to life.

Managers make sure the day-to-day work fits within the lines of the culture. They are the course-correctors and reinforcers. They are responsible for the day-to-day culture.

Managers are often put in the middle between aspirations and reality. But they also tend to be privy to the strategic and cultural context that employees are not. Because of that, managers are often able to help people come along in the culture journey by translating aspirations into the day-to-day work and showing people how important each of them is to the organisation.

How can managers be better culture translators?

1. Understand the aspirational culture at a behavioural level. What does demonstrating the aspirational culture look like in action?

2. Role model the culture. Show through their own behaviours how they would like their employees to behave.

3. Talk with people about why culture matters.

4. Guide and coach people to embody the culture. Make sure they understand how important their own actions are to making the culture come to life.

5. Build trust with their people and advocate for them.

6. Ask for resources and information they need to make the culture come to life. Help leaders understand the gaps in their experience in trying to translate and operationalise the culture. Do they need more training? More up-to-date information? More authority and latitude to support their people?

7. Tell stories about when people make the culture come to life or suffer because of it.

People

If leaders form and transform culture and managers course correct and reinforce, what role does everyone else play? Are they just innocent cultural bystanders or, worse yet, culture victims? And what about change from the bottom up – that beautiful idea where people create a movement and convince the organisation to make the changes they need in the culture?

I am a huge believer in self-efficacy, of individual humans

believing in themselves and taking action to make their circumstances better. That said, I don't think organisational culture can be transformed without the support of those with power. And the opposite can be said too. Leaders cannot mandate culture change from above. It takes the whole organisation.

Without your leaders on board, any kind of culture evolution is doomed to fail. But why? Given there are more people who make up the general employee base, it would seem this larger number of people would have more of a grassroots or bottom-up influence. In some rare cases, that does happen. But for most organisations, culture is shaped and transformed by those who hold power, which tends to be the founders and the most senior leaders of an organisation.

On top of that, the degree to which people without power can successfully impact the culture varies from company to company. As organisational psychologist Lindsay Bousman told me: "How realistic it is for employees to influence the culture has to do with the culture itself – it's a circular problem." If there's a history of grassroots efforts being adopted and reinforced, then it's possible for the momentum to build and to cause a movement to change the culture from the bottom up. But if that hasn't been the case, it will be an uphill battle for employees to work on culture change.

So what can you do about culture if you don't have positional power? First, you can build your organisational power in other ways. Consider the types of power outlined at the beginning of this chapter. A good place to start is by being an expert or by sharing information: share what you know about culture and why it matters. You can also work on referent power to build meaningful relationships with others so you can inspire them to also work on culture.

You might also work on identifying how your organisation distributes power. Organisations that are intentionally distributing their power, creating psychological safety and encouraging diverse perspectives and participation in decision making are more likely to have cultures that value human beings. If your organisation has power centred primarily in one or two people at the very top, it is likely to have a culture that is more about control. Control, at its core, is about fear. And fear-based cultures are not usually ones that value human beings.

This idea of power distribution and power sharing will impact someone's ability to change culture. If power is not shared, an individual employee's efforts to raise a flag about their culture concerns is not likely to go far. But if culture is more distributed, it is much more possible.

Employees *initiating* culture change without the help of leadership is possible. But for real change to continue to evolve after initiation, leaders are typically needed to ensure the change becomes part of the norm and power is shared with employees. Buurtzorg, a Dutch home healthcare organisation, experienced a culture change driven by its employees: the organisation has moved from a traditional hierarchical structure to a system based on self-managed teams.

People at Buurtzorg are now empowered to make decisions collectively and take ownership of their work. This shift has allowed them to provide better care to patients and has fostered a culture of trust, collaboration and innovation. The change was initiated and implemented by the employees themselves, leading to improved outcomes for both patients and employees.[12] It's a good example of positive bottom-up change in action: employees initiated the change and leaders then empowered employees to make it happen by supporting them to take ownership and make decisions.

Similarly, Morning Star, a leading tomato-processing company based in California, transformed its culture through self-management practices. The organisation implemented a system called Colleague Principles that empowers employees to make decisions without traditional hierarchies. Employees at Morning Star are responsible for defining their roles, setting goals and managing their work relationships. This employee-driven culture change allows individuals to take ownership of their work, collaborate effectively and drive innovation.[13] Those in positions of power at Morning Star have decided to adopt self-management as their core management philosophy – another great example of power sharing that is supported by those with the most power.

How can people influence culture?

1. Vote with their hands. Raise their hands about what's not working. Provide specific feedback about how the culture is hindering or helping progress.

2. Do more of what is working within the culture, build on and call out the aspects of the culture that are helping the organisation move forward.

3. Tell managers and leaders about how people are impacted by the culture.

4. Bring solutions. Offer ideas for how to improve the culture.

5. Get clear about their own values and how they mesh (or don't) with the organisation's. This clarity will help them be more intentional about how they experience their organisation's culture.

6. Vote with their feet. If the culture is toxic, they should leave. Find another organisation that is more intentional about its culture.

Power, culture and inclusion

With power comes bias. Those in the organisation who do not share the same set of values, beliefs and priorities as those in power may find themselves at odds with cultural expectations. And because senior leaders tend to be older, white and male, the culture of many organisations is formed by their experiences and what they deem important.

Similarly, most founders of companies are also white and male. For example, the majority of founders of tech companies in the United States (77%)[14] and Europe (84%)[15] are white or Caucasian. And only 36% of US founders are women.[16] In a worldwide sample, the average of female founders (the total number of female founders divided by the number of start-up founders surveyed) is just 15%.[17] So the deeply rooted aspects of culture that originate with founders may value very different things to what the organisation's current employees value.

I remember working on an intense project with a CEO, where we were together for long periods of time. After working on the project all day and during one of our breaks, I said out loud what I was thinking: "What am I going to make for dinner tonight?" He looked at me, perplexed. He said that he never had to think about that as his wife always took care of dinner every night. At the time, I had two small kids at home and always felt like there weren't enough hours in the day. I remember feeling resentful and that there was no way he understood what I was going through (with something as simple as dinner, much less the bigger challenges).

Routinely, he would emphasise how important it was to grind, to kill it, to win. I often felt like I understood why he felt like we had to "grind" (work hard, work long hours), but it felt quite impossible to live up to those expectations as a working mum.

Being a working mum is just one example of a disconnect with white male-dominated leadership that forms cultures. Of course, other underrepresented identifiers such as race, physical ability, sexuality and neuroability can also come into conflict with a set of values created by leaders. Employees who have different identities and experiences may find that some aspects of their organisation's culture go against their own values or at least are not in line with how they want to work.

In recent years, the US National Football League (NFL) has been a classic example of how people who are in positions of power in a white male-dominated culture can cause serious damage. Multiple incidents have been reported involving the mistreatment of women, black and other underrepresented employees within the league. In a *New York Times* article, more than 30 women spoke about their experiences working for the NFL, describing a corporate culture that demoralises female employees and disregards their concerns.[18] Employees reported bias, inadequate training and little or no support when they raised issues. And once issues were raised, the NFL did not terminate the contracts of senior level executives who were mistreating employees.

This lack of action sends a clear message to employees: those in a position of power can do what they want, without fear of consequences. It also sends a message about what is really valued in the culture: not the "respect" and "integrity" on their website, but instead protecting the powerful.

Creating more inclusion

Some organisations have added diversity and inclusion-related values to their "aspire to" culture, which is a step in the right direction. This at least puts a spotlight on the aspiration of inclusion. Of course, the ideas underlying this value must be enacted and embedded. It can't just be surface-level or a tick-box approach.

Organisations also need to continue to dig into how the social identities of those in positions of power influence cultural norms that might, at their core, be holding back the organisation and its people from reaching their full potential. They might even be a source of systemic bias. These social identities, such as race, gender and ethnicity, can shape individuals' perspectives, values and decision-making processes, which can inadvertently perpetuate existing power imbalances and reinforce biases.

It takes critical self-reflection and proactive steps to identify and challenge the underlying assumptions and biases that may exist within power structures. This includes fostering awareness of privilege (special advantages that some groups have over others) and leveraging the power of those in leadership positions to champion diversity, equity and inclusion.[19]

There are, however, a range of things that organisations can do to create more inclusive cultures.

Hiring and retention

Hire (and retain) people who represent diverse perspectives and backgrounds and put them in positions of power. Challenge the "stale, male and pale" traditions of leadership and hire people using new and different recruiting sources than previously.

Actively create safe spaces

Next, work on embedding more psychological safety in your organisation, ensuring that people feel comfortable speaking up even when it is difficult or goes against the status quo. Focusing on psychological safety is much more than offering a training class. As HR leader Sarah Stevens told me: "It's not enough to just say this is a safe space. You have to go out of your way to determine what creates a safe space for each person – there's a lot of work and actions you need to take." Psychological safety will help ensure that diverse perspectives are included – but it needs to be actively and intentionally created.

A great example of how values and diversity can work together comes from Clotia Robinson, an organisational consultant who worked at the Seattle Public Library. One of her responsibilities was to help enhance the library's service delivery environment. The library system is a rich, culturally diverse setting, both in terms of its employees and the public it serves. At the time, the library had just developed new organisational values that needed to be rolled out. Clotia was acutely aware of how important it was to incorporate them into everything they did in the library.

Clotia also decided to connect the dots between the organisational values and the personal and cultural values of the employees of the library system. She knew she needed to focus on helping everyone build the knowledge, skills and abilities to serve a culturally and racially diverse public.

At the time, the library had 700 employees dispersed across 27 locations speaking 30 different languages. Clotia had the idea of having employees run the sessions about the organisational values through their own individual lenses. She called these sessions Our Way. Team members presented during lunch and learn sessions, discussing how the library's values intersected with their own personal values as well as their own ethnic and national/geographical values.

Being proactive about creating spaces where people could talk about their own identities and experiences worked. These sessions were extremely well received. Not only were the new values rolled out, but team members also got to know each other better and, once they learned more about the backgrounds and values of the people they worked with and served, developed more empathy towards them. Another benefit was that the people who volunteered to do the sessions felt they were learning and growing too, by having the opportunity to prepare and present in front of others.

Distributing power

Another step is to closely examine how your organisation distributes power. The idea of employee empowerment explores how power is distributed throughout organisations. Can employees make decisions, especially decisions related to their own roles? What decisions can frontline managers make? Most organisations do a poor job at understanding how power is distributed. But decentralisation of power can help employees feel like they matter and are trusted and valued.

Studies have shown that decentralised power structures, where decision-making authority is distributed among employees at various levels, can lead to higher levels of employee autonomy and empowerment.[20] This, in turn, fosters a sense of ownership and commitment among employees, as they have a greater say in shaping their work environment and influencing organisational outcomes.[21]

Power sharing can also have positive effects on creativity and innovation within organisations. When employees perceive higher levels of decision-making power and autonomy, they are more likely to engage in innovative behaviours and contribute novel ideas.[22]

Mentoring and sponsorship

Organisations can also foster inclusion by implementing mentoring and sponsorship programmes. These programmes can provide support and guidance to underrepresented individuals within the organisation, helping them navigate the complexities of their careers and providing opportunities for advancement. Mentoring relationships enable knowledge transfer and skill development, whereas sponsorship programmes are about advocacy and visibility. Both are important.

Leadership behaviour

Leadership behaviour is crucial to inclusion. Leaders must be role models for listening and actively enquiring and seeking to understand others. They cannot force their opinions into every conversation. In most cases, leaders should speak last, acknowledging and appreciating the input of others and reinforcing the good ideas generated by them.

Some organisations are putting concrete plans forward to improve in this area. Google, for example, has faced criticism about its lack of diversity and inclusion. In 2014, the company released its diversity data, revealing a significant underrepresentation of women and underrepresented groups in its workforce, especially in technical and leadership roles. This lack of diversity raised concerns about the company's commitment to inclusion and its ability to address the needs of a large and diverse user base.

The release of this data became the catalyst for action; Google put various initiatives in place to improve diversity and inclusion. They implemented unconscious bias training programmes to educate employees about implicit biases affecting decision-making processes. They also established employee resource groups (ERGs) to provide support and networking opportunities for underrepresented groups.

To hold leaders accountable, Google tied executive bonuses to diversity and inclusion goals. The idea was to incentivise leaders to prioritise diversity in their hiring practices and promote an inclusive culture. The company also expanded its recruiting efforts to reach a more diverse talent pool, partnering with organisations focused on underrepresented groups.

Google also announced the establishment of a $175m racial equity initiative aimed at supporting Black-owned businesses, entrepreneurs and start-ups, as well as investing in educational and career opportunities for underrepresented communities. It also set a target to improve the representation of underrepresented groups, particularly Black employees, at the leadership level.[23] And it continues to work on making further improvement, publishing annual diversity reports with specific actions that it's taking to improve diversity and inclusion.[24]

The jury is still out as to whether Google will be committed for the long run and whether its efforts will influence the day-to-day employee experience of the culture. For example, the effectiveness of unconscious bias training has been challenged, as has putting the onus for change on underrepresented groups to run ERGs, many times without additional compensation.

But the intention is there. More organisations need to recognise the power dynamics at play when it comes to positive cultures that support diversity and inclusion.

Organisational power and culture are deeply connected. Power within an organisation influences the development, maintenance and manifestation of its culture. The distribution of power, the types of power wielded by individuals, and the way in which power is exercised all shape the norms, values, beliefs and behaviours that define the culture. And power, culture and inclusion are all interrelated. Recognising and understanding these relationships is vital for anyone seeking to create a positive and effective work environment.

Remember

1. To understand culture, understand power. Power and culture go hand in hand.

2. When people are learning about culture, they look to those who have made it to understand what is valued in the organisation. These are typically people who are in positions of power.

3. Positional, referent, informational, expert, reward and coercive power are different types of power that can be present in organisations.

4. Leaders, founders, managers and boards need to understand how their power influences the behaviour of employees and should take proactive steps to create more inclusive cultures.

5. Organisations need to understand how the social identities of those in positions of power influence cultural norms that might be holding back the organisation and its people from reaching their full potential.

6. Everyone at work has power. But it's important to understand how power is distributed and how it impacts our organisation's culture if we are to understand the extent to which employees can influence it.

The future of culture means we will get smarter about culture and question some of the assumptions we have made about it. The next chapter pinpoints some of the most important assumptions we have about culture and how we might think differently about culture in the future.

PART 3

The future of culture

Overview

In Part 2, I explored how to know when your organisation is ready to evolve its culture and how to do so using the Intentional Culture Circle. I also covered a critical component to culture evolution – organisational power.

In Part 3, I look at the future of culture. In Chapter 8, I discuss the need for us to question many of the assumptions we have had in the past about culture and suggest new ways we might think about culture by introducing nine cultural assumptions that need re-evaluation. The assumptions range from the belief that culture takes a back seat when employees are being offered a promotion to the idea that organisations should seek one overarching culture.

In Chapter 9, the last chapter of the book, I suggest an important viewpoint for future culture – that maybe we should not be agnostic about what type of culture an organisation should have provided it is aligned with its business strategy (a belief I used to have). I now believe that at least some aspects of an organisation's culture should be focused on valuing human beings. For business strategies to thrive, an organisational culture should prioritise the values associated with being human, such as caring for the whole person, inclusion, belonging, integrity, compassion and kindness. I introduce the concept of Culture Care Stairs, a framework delineating three levels of cultural progression. The last part of Chapter 9 delves into the "hearts" component of hearts and minds, exploring emotions at work, personal values, human connection and purpose.

8

Rethinking cultural assumptions

Understanding yourself and what you value is a first step in finding a culture that works for you. Sophie, a business consultant in France, is a great example of someone who is clear about what she values – but this has only happened over time and through some challenging situations.

Fourteen years ago, Sophie was working in a large consulting company in Paris. When she was pregnant with her third child, she found out that she was being considered for a promotion to principal consultant. At the same time, she was also approached by a senior leader, a woman, who told her that Sophie now had to choose between her career or her family, as she had done: either Sophie should turn down the chance of promotion or give up her aspiration to be a mum who was around for her children. After hearing her out, Sophie decided to ignore her and formally applied for the promotion anyway, determined not to give up on any part of her life.

Sophie got the promotion. But it came with a not-so-subtle string attached: her promotion would feature in a public relations campaign to showcase the support of the company for working mothers.

Sophie was disgusted. She did not feel that the culture was flexible or that she had received much support as a working mum. She was troubled by the "choice" that the senior leader had given her, and the lack of flexibility in assignments. It didn't seem that leaders were on board with supporting working mothers.

Sophie decided that her own values, which prioritised her family and involved flexibility, went against the values of the organisation. But she was especially concerned with the organisation wanting to create a false picture of what was happening by using her as a mouthpiece for something that wasn't true; her integrity means a lot to her. Sophie left that organisation and thinks that her experience there helped her to get clear about what matters to her and to find another organisation that is more aligned with what she believes in.

When there's a disconnect between personal values and organisational values, there are real implications. For Sophie, this disconnect was big enough and important enough for her to take action and leave.

In this chapter, I explore some of the assumptions we have made about culture and why we should think differently about them, starting with why we need to rethink our assumptions that culture is of secondary importance. As the example with Sophie demonstrates, when it comes to a conflict between personal and organisational values, many people make the decision to leave, even when offered a promotion.

Here are nine assumptions about culture that need to be understood and challenged if culture is to become a force for good.

Assumption about culture	But actually
If employees are promoted or paid more, culture takes a back seat	Value disconnects can cause cognitive dissonance that people often would rather reconcile by leaving than stay with the values disconnect and receive more rewards.
An organisation needs one overarching culture that everyone must adhere to	The organisation should decide if unification across the organisation is necessary. And if it is, which aspects of the culture need to be shared across the organisation and how flexibility across geographies and identities can be embraced.
If done right, culture rarely changes	Culture should change as the environment and conditions change.
Organisations should look for people who are the best culture fit	Culture fit can create too much similarity in an organisation. Look for people who embrace the core aspects of the culture, but who also provide unique perspectives and talents.
Values are the best way to drive culture	Values are a great way to create a focus on the most important aspects of the culture. But they need to be accompanied with aligned behaviours, practices and systems.
It doesn't matter if I'm not aligned with my company's values – it's just a job	It is very difficult to compartmentalise work from life outside work. This disconnect between personal and work values will create issues in the short term and long term.
The only way to change the culture is to understand what the culture is	Understanding how well an organisation's culture is "working" may be a better approach.
Understanding culture is simple	Culture is complex, elusive and multifaceted. But that should not hold us back from seeking to understand it and to be more intentional about it.
Because work is changing so much, culture will become increasingly irrelevant	As we go through a radical change in what work is and how it is accomplished, culture will be more relevant than ever.

Assumption 1. If employees are promoted or paid more, culture takes a back seat

As Sophie's example demonstrates, the disconnect between personal values and what the organisation values can create cognitive dissonance, the discomfort people feel when there is a contradiction between different beliefs or between beliefs and actions. This can lead to feelings of inner conflict, confusion and stress as people try to reconcile the differences. The desire *not* to feel this way often becomes more important than the desire to receive a promotion or a bonus.

Research into employee attrition backs this up; compensation only moderately impacts the way people feel about where they work.[1] The largest predictor of attrition was toxic culture (which was ranked number 1), followed by job insecurity and reorganisation.

So, a bad culture isn't something you can just throw more money at. Eventually, a bad culture catches up with you. And employees won't wait around for organisations to turn it around. I find it interesting that if toxic culture is the most important driver of attrition, why don't we have more organisational accountability for it? Conceptually, culture is everyone's job, but unfortunately, in practice, that often means that culture is no one's job.

Challenging this assumption means you take culture seriously and have intentional plans and responsible parties to work on it.

Assumption 2. An organisation needs one overarching culture that everyone must adhere to

Another common assumption is that everyone within an organisation should share the same values, beliefs and work attitudes. Similarly, some people also assume that an organisation's culture is uniform across all departments or divisions. However, this assumption is often untrue. Organisations are made up of diverse individuals with varying backgrounds, experiences and perspectives – and this is a good thing. Different departments within an organisation can develop their own subcultures based on their own functions, goals and leadership styles.

What is more important is that the organisation decides the fundamental things that need to be shared and universally understood. And then, outside that core, focus on what matters most; the organisation can offer flexibility and localisation for everything else.

Some organisations have been built through acquisition. It should not necessarily be assumed that the organisation should have a set of shared values across the acquired companies. Is there a business reason for the organisation to be unified? Do the companies acquired need to accomplish something together? Think through whether unification across departments, divisions or geographies is critical to success. If it is, determine which specific aspects of the culture need to be shared across the organisation and how flexibility across geographies and identities can be embraced.

Challenging this assumption requires us all to have a more nuanced understanding of organisational culture: understanding which aspects of culture are core and need to be shared, and which are dynamic and should be different.

Assumption 3. If done right, culture rarely changes

Another assumption is that organisational culture remains stable and consistent. In reality, organisational culture is not static. It can (and should) evolve with changes in leadership, major shifts in strategic goals, mergers and other external influences. What might have been true about the culture a few years ago might not hold true today. And what is true today might not work for what we need tomorrow. Culture needs to flex.

It's important to know how you'll assess whether your culture is still working for you or not. That doesn't mean that your culture focus should change every year. The culture should be thought of as stable and principled but also able to adapt to both internal and external changes as necessary.

Unfortunately, the assumption that culture rarely changes can lead to people feeling blindsided when they realise that the culture they joined (and which may have been a primary reason they joined) is changing, causing potential disillusionment. In one company I worked with, the employee base had been through a few years of constant change when I was hired to help the company develop its aspirational culture. The people there wanted to hold onto the existing culture. We spent a lot of time discussing why some aspects of the culture needed to change, given the big strategic shifts that were happening. We also worked to keep some of the key ideas that still held true from the existing culture as we were developing our plans for the future.

Organisations must be able to adapt to changing circumstances, and one of the most important systems that needs to align with these changes is culture.

Assumption 4. Organisations should look for people who are the best culture fit

Get on the bus. Be a team player. Fit in or f*** off.

These are all terms that, assuming positive intent, are meant to unify and to drive high performance. There's logic in identifying the aspirational culture, finding candidates who want to be part of it, and encouraging existing employees to buy into it.

Many companies have focused on people who fit in with their culture. Unfortunately, some of these companies have used this idea of culture fit to hire, promote and retain people they are comfortable with, who look like them and who act like them – more of a comfort fit than a culture fit. Lauren Rivera, an associate professor of management and organisations at Northwestern University, Illinois, calls this "looking glass merit", the idea that people unconsciously define a candidate's worthiness as a potential employee in a way that is self-validating.[2] In other words, if I see myself in you, you must be great (because I'm great); you will fit in here (because I do).

There is a real downside to hiring only people you are comfortable with. When you are comfortable, you might not hear other perspectives or try new things. And this is a slippery slope into hiring people with the same background, gender, race, ethnicity, age, ability and sexual orientation. Using the culture fit approach, before long, you have a company full of people who look the same and act the same – and sameness is not cultural alignment. A lack of diversity in thought and background can inhibit an organisation's ability to adapt to complex and rapidly changing environments.

As individuals, people who are aware of their own norms, values and beliefs have a better chance of finding a match with their next company's culture. Unfortunately, most people have not had the opportunity to understand their own values, especially how that relates to their work. So before you can know whether a company's culture is the right one for you, you must first understand what you yourself value.

But don't be too rigid in trying to find an exact fit between what you value and the company you are looking to join. Instead, look for companies that will value what you uniquely bring to the table and that aren't asking you to conform to a narrow definition of professionalism or success.

One way to think about this is finding a company that has a healthy balance of "we" and "me". In other words, there is a desire to unify employees to something bigger in the organisation that is attractive to you (the "we"), but there is also an emphasis explicitly placed on *you being you* (the "me").

Instead of focusing on culture fit, some organisations have adopted the idea of "culture add" – finding candidates who share the same core values but also bring something else to the organisation, making the culture better. This is more of an idea of culture expansion than a rigid, "colour between the lines" one that the culture fit approach can reinforce. A focus on "culture add" is a healthy way for an organisation to be flexible and adaptive but still stay true to its core values.

Assumption 5. Values are the best way to drive culture

Throughout this book, I've talked about the importance of organisational values. Articulating values helps create clarity about what matters the most. But values alone are not the best way to drive culture. As we saw in Chapter 5, they need to be clearly defined and described in behavioural terms – that is, behaviouralised. They must also be embedded in organisational systems and practices.

I was once in a client's leadership meeting, reviewing the results of an employee survey with them. Some of the items on the survey were related to the culture and specifically how well each of their values was being demonstrated by employees, managers and leaders.

After seeing that the results were quite low for many of their values, the CEO said that he wasn't surprised, that even he didn't understand what the values meant. So what's the chance that employees understood them or that they could be demonstrated more widely? He agreed that one of the most important actions from the survey was to define and create behaviours for each of their values more explicitly.

Values need to be connected to strategy, behaviouralised, reinforced, communicated and woven into the practices and systems of the business. In other words, they have to be alive and real.

Assumption 6. It doesn't matter if I'm not aligned with my company's values – it's just a job

Feeling misalignment between personal values and your organisation's values can be profoundly disconcerting. Our personal values are a fundamental aspect of our identity, shaping our beliefs, decisions and interactions. When these values clash with those upheld by the organisation we work for, it can create a deep sense of internal conflict.

The challenge arises from the difficulty in compartmentalising two parts of our life that are misaligned. Human beings don't neatly separate their personal and professional lives; they are inherently intertwined. Attempting to suppress or disregard personal values to align with the organisation's values can lead to emotional distress, cognitive dissonance and a loss of authenticity.

The impact of trying to push through this misalignment between personal and organisational values can be multifaceted and severe. At an emotional level, this internal discord can result in heightened stress, anxiety and even feelings of depression. And the effort to maintain a façade of conformity can be mentally draining, leading to burnout and a diminished sense of self-worth.

Over time, this can erode your passion and enthusiasm for work, as the struggle to find meaning in tasks can seem at odds with your core beliefs. This strain may extend to personal relationships, and as you try to reconcile your conflicting values it can spill over into interactions with family and friends.

At work, the consequences can be equally damaging. Someone dealing with this kind of misalignment might find it difficult to fully engage in their job, reducing their productivity. This lack of authenticity can also get in the way of effective communication, as you might hesitate to express ideas or concerns that deviate from the organisation's norms. This might mean that you withdraw and are not participating fully at work.

Ultimately, the organisation itself stands to lose, as disenchanted employees are more likely to disengage, become outspoken critics of the culture, or leave. Being misaligned on a values level with your organisation isn't something you can fake for very long – eventually it catches up with you.

Assumption 7. The only way to change the culture is to understand what the culture is

One of the natural first steps of culture work is to start digging into cultural attributes; that is, deciding which words best describe the culture. But there are lots of challenges when trying to describe what that culture might be. People may be so immersed in the culture that they might not be able to see it or describe it. Culture can be so abstract that you might not be able to find the words that adequately describe it. And culture is so tightly related to organisational purpose, strategy and the external ecosystem that it is hard to create uniform ways of talking about and measuring it across organisations. There aren't well-accepted off-the-shelf measures of culture that organisations can easily use to bypass these issues.

So instead of trying to dig into culture by finding the words to describe and measure it, another approach is to start by ascertaining the extent to which the culture is *working*.

For instance, you could ask the following questions.

- Is the culture aligned with strategy/vision/mission/ purpose?
- Do people understand what is really valued in this organisation?
- Is there clarity about the culture the organisation aspires to have?
- Do people understand what the cultural expectations are?
- Do people understand what the values look like in action?
- Do people feel connected with each other?
- Do people feel connected to the organisation?
- Do people feel inspired by the strategy/vision/mission/ purpose and culture?
- Is the culture intentional and embedded throughout the organisation?
- Is there a uniform experience of the culture?

These questions can be part of employee focus groups or workshops, or they can be included in employee surveys (ideally, both qualitative and quantitative methods are used). Results will offer new insights in terms of what's working well with the culture and where there are gaps.

This approach helps you to know how well your current focus on culture is working and whether the culture is being optimised. You may then decide to move on to think about cultural attributes, but exploring how well the culture is working can be a straightforward place to start.

Assumption 8. Understanding culture is simple

Although much of this book is aimed at trying to make culture understandable and approachable for everyone, that should not be confused with thinking that culture is simple. Culture is complex, multifaceted, elusive and ever-changing.

Most organisations have a short attention span, a desire to simplify big problems into three bullet points on a PowerPoint slide. There's little patience for sitting in complexity and ambiguity. Instead, there's a push for next steps and action plans. As cognitive anthropologist David White said, where we get to is "a culture construct reduced to the most basic terms so it can be easily consumed by an impatient and pragmatic audience interested primarily in expedience". [3]

But because culture is so important and so powerful, you can't be paralysed by its complexity or so caught up in theoretical discussions that you don't take the actions needed to make culture better for the people who are being impacted by it every day. Instead, try to find approaches and methodologies that acknowledge this complexity but also help you to make progress.

You can use the Intentional Culture Circle outlined earlier in this book (see page 83) to find a way to start.

Assumption 9. Because work is changing so much, culture will become increasingly irrelevant

The dynamic landscape of work – marked by everything from artificial intelligence (AI), gig work and innovative organisational structures like decentralised autonomous organisations (DAOs) – is reshaping the importance of organisational culture in profound ways.

As technology accelerates the pace of change, traditional hierarchical structures are giving way to more agile, decentralised models. In this context, organisational culture can be the unifying force that creates a sense of belonging and purpose, even in the absence of direct supervision. And as AI takes over routine tasks and gig workers contribute their specialised skills for short-term projects, culture becomes crucial for ensuring cohesion and direction.

While perhaps improving efficiency, AI can also create a sense of detachment among employees. The incorporation of AI-driven processes requires a new focus on values that create a sense of shared identity and connection. Organisational culture can bridge this gap by emphasising these human values that AI cannot easily replicate, such as respect, integrity, compassion and purpose.

Gig work demands a culture that can quickly integrate the perspectives and talents of its members who may not naturally feel connected to each other. A clear and intentional culture can serve as a unifying force that transcends this disconnection, creating a sense of community and belonging.

The rise of new organisational models like DAOs presents a major shift that underscores the importance of culture. When geographical boundaries are less relevant and DAO contributors span the globe, culture serves as the glue that binds members together and guides their collective decisions. The culture of a DAO becomes its identity, driving participation, commitment and a shared sense of ownership.

Among all these (and other) transformative changes to work, organisational culture acts as a stabilising force, providing a sense of continuity amid disruption. It's the cultural fabric that allows employees to find meaning and coherence in their roles, even as the nature of work evolves.

As these new forces reshape work, the question is not whether culture will remain relevant, but how organisations can intentionally craft and cultivate their cultures to navigate these changes successfully.

*

As these assumptions show, there's a lot for us to understand about culture. We must continue to evolve our understanding and become more comfortable about the grey area that culture sits in – it is about nuance and "maybe" rather than "yes or no" or "either this or that". Our continued curiosity about culture and our evolving understanding are what will help to ensure a future where everyone not only understands the importance of culture, but also understands how to improve it.

Remember

1. When personal values and organisational values are at odds, there are real consequences to the people experiencing this disconnect.

2. Culture needs to flex. It should adapt as the organisation changes. Employees should not all have to be the same or act the same, but there should be a core culture that helps to unify.

3. It's important to understand how well the culture is working for the organisation.

4. Culture work cannot stop with just developing values. Values need to be accompanied by behaviours, practices and systems.

5. As the world of work changes, the human values that underpin organisational culture will become more important.

Culture is complex, elusive and multifaceted – just like the humans who create it. And just like the humans who create culture, there is unlimited potential to evolve your understanding of culture and make work better. In the final chapter, I look at how organisations can prioritise the humans who are so critical to their cultures and their success.

9

Valuing humans

In her role as a senior project manager at a multinational corporation, working out of its Quebec office, Stephanie was a key player in using design thinking to help with new product ideation and innovation. After being with the company for a few years, she had the opportunity to design a collaborative project between her company and a local university, with manifold benefits for the company, its clients and the students. Stephanie had the idea of creating an all-day design thinking experience for a group of MBA students, and she and a colleague worked many overtime hours to make the idea happen.

At the same time, the company was strongly advocating for the value of building connections between its own internal departments, and this project was an opportunity for Stephanie to do just that. Historically, there was little interaction between the separate departments and her project management responsibilities. But with this university project, she was able to bring together multiple internal teams and showcase this collaboration, which was very much in line with the values espoused by the company at the time.

The project was a huge success. The students' feedback was that it was one of the most exciting experiences they had had as part of their courses. Because of this success, the company planned a second phase of the same project with the university.

It was during this launch of the second phase of the project that a senior leader from another department became involved. This leader was initially not interested at all, but when the company's Chief Design Officer started to take notice, she used the leverage of her higher position to take charge of the project and removed Stephanie from the equation, with no explanation.

"I became totally demoralised and completely disengaged from that point forward," Stephanie relates. She tried to escalate her frustrations up the chain of command with the help of her own manager and the colleague with whom she worked on the project. Because she was in one department and the leader who took over the project was in another, nobody seemed to be able or willing to address her concerns, which were passed around from one supervisor to another and never went anywhere.

Stephanie says she thinks this is because ultimately the true culture that was valued was not one of cross-department collaboration or building bridges like the company had talked about, but rather a "culture of deferring to and rewarding those in higher positions". She says: "It matters more where you sit in the hierarchy than your actual accomplishments, and too many people feel their reputations are at stake if they rock the boat. They won't go out on a limb for someone in a subordinate position."

In the end, she was told to drop it and get back to work. Even when she involved HR, the only suggestion was that she go to her employee assistance programme for counselling. In the face of this, she became depressed and it took her nine months to get back into the swing of things at work.

Stephanie's example is a real one. And similar scenarios play out every day where culture impacts real people. Of course, these situations are complicated and are rarely clear cut. It was easy for this organisation to blame Stephanie and leave her isolated, instead of owning up to its culture being at the root of the issue. Perhaps if the leaders had more clarity and commitment to their people, this situation could have been avoided.

Human-centred culture

One of this book's core messages is that culture needs to be aligned with business strategy. But what about the importance of people in that strategy?

Without people who are dedicated and committed, it's difficult for most business strategies to succeed. And because most companies also have human beings as customers or consumers, valuing humans should be a priority for any organisation's culture.

The idea is that cultural values should have at their core a set of more universally adopted human cultural attributes – and not just operational ones. These should include things like caring for the whole human being, inclusion, belonging, integrity, compassion and kindness. I believe that every organisation's values should focus on the human aspects of their culture.

That doesn't mean that this will automatically be the case. Organisations will be at different stages of this journey. For some, basic respect needs to be emphasised. Others will have made significant progress and have higher aspirations – for example, they may decide to focus more on how they can have a positive impact on the world.

This progression is represented by the Culture Care Stairs shown in Figure 11. The stairs offer a map for organisations to plot where they are in terms of valuing and caring for people and how they can aspire to the different levels. The ideas here

Figure 11: **Culture care stairs**

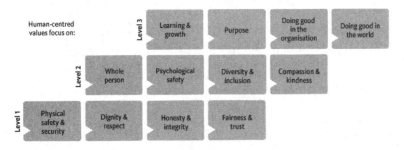

can be seen as potential culture attributes to be included in the aspirational culture you are creating.

Level 1

The first level focuses on fundamentals, starting with basic physical safety and security, dignity and respect, honesty and integrity, fairness and trust. These values are the foundation of a culture. Without these in place and experienced by employees, it's hard to go further on your culture journey.

- **Physical safety and security:** prioritising measures and protocols that create a work environment free from potential harm or danger. This includes implementing safeguards, training and policies that address risks and ensure that employees are physically safe.

- **Dignity and respect:** treating everyone with basic human consideration, irrespective of their role or background. It involves fostering an atmosphere where each employee's worth is acknowledged and upheld.

- **Honesty and integrity:** encouraging and expecting consistent truthfulness and ethical behaviour in all interactions and decisions. This commitment involves promoting transparency, accountability and a strong moral compass within the culture.

- **Fairness and trust:** ensuring everyone is treated equitably and without bias, that opportunities are distributed impartially and that there are consistent and just practices in the organisation.

Level 2

Level 2 builds on the fundamentals of Level 1, focusing more on treating people well, seeing them as entire human beings and valuing them for who they are. It's also about creating an environment where people feel comfortable to be themselves and speak up for what they need.

- **Whole person:** a recognition of people's needs, whether professional, personal or in terms of their well-being. This approach allows individuals to thrive both professionally and personally, acknowledging the interconnectedness of their lives inside and outside work.

- **Psychological safety:** cultivating an environment where employees feel comfortable expressing their thoughts, ideas and concerns without fear of negative consequences. With psychological safety, employees can be themselves; they don't have to hold back or be someone they aren't.

- **Diversity and inclusion:** recognising and embracing the varied backgrounds, perspectives and experiences that employees bring to the table and actively creating an environment where all individuals feel respected, empowered and able to contribute authentically.

- **Compassion and kindness:** valuing how employees treat each other, focusing on being kind and supportive and creating an empathetic culture so that those who work in the organisation want to take action to help each other.

Level 3

The top level of the stairs is about creating a higher purpose and having a positive impact on people both within and outside the organisation. At this level, there is a higher-level focus on creating good in the world.

- **Learning and growth:** prioritising opportunities for employees to continually develop their skills, knowledge and capabilities.

- **Connecting employees to purpose:** helping your employees connect to a deeper sense of purpose is a way to show employees that you value them and care about them as human beings.

- **Doing good in the organisation:** demonstrating through your actions that you want to support employees by helping them during times of need or supporting them in their life outside work. It's also about minimising the impact of the organisation on the environment and implementing sustainable practices internally.

- **Doing good in the world:** signifies an organisation's commitment to making a positive impact beyond its immediate operations by engaging in socially responsible and ethical practices. This includes initiatives that contribute to the betterment of society, the environment and communities, demonstrating a broader commitment to corporate social responsibility.

Every organisation has different markets, strategies and priorities and may have various reasons for progressing at different speeds on the journey of valuing human beings. The Culture Care Stairs can help you think about where you are now and where you might want to go next. The important thing is to be intentional about making a start.

The "hearts" of hearts and minds

Earlier, I shared the idea that a focus on culture means a focus on hearts and minds.

The "minds" aspect is about the data, logic and methodology of culture work: how we measure culture, how we break it down, the logical steps we take to form and transform it.

The "hearts" comprises four important areas:

- emotions at work
- personal values
- human connection
- purpose.

Emotions at work

> This is business, I don't care about your feelings.
> Keep emotions out of work.
> You can't make good decisions if you use your emotions.
> You are being too emotional.

Increasingly, we realise how ridiculous those statements are and how much this way of thinking holds people back in understanding how to use emotions constructively at work. Completely dismissing emotions has stunted our understanding of how to use them productively in the workplace. Some organisations send mixed signals to employees by offering emotional intelligence courses for managers and leaders, but then chastising employees when they display emotions at work. This is confusing and often feels disingenuous, leaving employees to wonder whether the organisation cares about how they feel.

It's easy to think about how emotions can negatively impact what happens at work (think gossip, quiet quitting, burnout). But they can positively impact what happens at work too (feelings of engagement, well-being and joy). And because emotions are simply signals to pay attention, if they are dismissed at work, there's the chance that you are missing the important information that emotions are trying to tell you. Furthermore, we cannot expect people at work to compartmentalise themselves into *myself at work* and *myself outside work*. As we've seen, a disconnect between the two will often have negative consequences.

This disconnect between how a person really feels and how they need to pretend to feel is even more marked when the job requires a person to display emotions in a certain way, for example, smiling and being cheerful in a retail or service role. This concept is called emotional labour, and it describes the process of managing emotions in line with organisational display rules (eg, greeting every customer with a smile), even if they do not genuinely reflect a person's true feelings.[1] Emotional labour also can apply to managers and leaders who are trying to keep a calm demeanour during turbulent times. It can lead to emotional exhaustion and burnout, especially where employees frequently interact with customers or in organisations that experience a lot of chaos and change.

The sales representatives at American Express Company's life insurance division faced these emotional labour challenges while selling life insurance.[2] Clients often responded with fear, suspicion and anger, eroding employee morale and hindering sales. To tackle these issues, Kate Cannon, a former American

Express employee, used emotional resonance: a process to identify how employees' feelings about their work and about their clients created obstacles. For example, clients' negative emotions were not only impeding sales but also affecting the sales representatives, causing feelings of incompetence, shame and dishonesty.

Cannon discovered that the people who empathised with clients and aligned their feelings with their work were more successful. So she implemented an emotional awareness training programme for a test group of salespeople, aiming to help them understand and use their emotions better.

The programme had a significant positive impact, improving coping skills and leading to a substantial increase in sales. It proved that recognising and managing emotions can enhance both employee satisfaction and company profits. Rather than telling the salespeople to shut off their feelings or that their feelings didn't matter, they were supported to become more aware of their feelings and to use empathy to connect with their clients in a deeper way.

There are many levels of emotions at work.[3] We tend to think about emotions at the individual personal level – a person's own discrete emotions. But there's also how an individual person's emotions and styles intersect with another person's emotions and style; how groups or teams display emotion or have emotional norms; how managers and leaders demonstrate emotion or support those who do; and how much psychological safety there is to encourage people to be honest about how they feel at work.

The implication for culture work is that embracing emotions and giving people opportunities to feel what they feel can help them let go of the past and face the future. It's especially important not to negate the way people are feeling. If you want the energy of the positive emotions, you need to give people the opportunity to process and use less positive emotions too.

Personal values

To understand the human in a human-centred work culture, the humans must understand themselves. That means spending time with yourself to understand your own personal values, answering questions like: what matters the most to me and what do I stand for? Without this understanding, it will be difficult to understand whether an organisation's culture is the right one for you or not.

Most people have not done that self-reflection work. And those who do often do it when something dramatic or traumatic has happened in their lives. Imagine if we thought about what really matters to us before we started thinking about our careers?

There needs to be alignment between your personal values and the values of where you work. Your personal values can impact your work in multiple ways – in what work you choose to do (the actual content of your career), in how you do your work, and in where you decide to work. For example, you might have a personal value related to justice. You might take that personal value and choose to be an attorney, focused on defending people who have been wrongly accused. Or you might choose another career altogether, but in doing your work, you are aware of being fair and equitable with everyone you work with. Or you might decide that you want to work in an organisation that works in a similar way and values fairness and equity implicitly and explicitly through its values.

I had the opportunity to talk to someone who had this idea and then decided to do something about it. She's a brand strategist named Andreea Niculescu, and she partnered with the artist Lisa Congdon to create a set of values cards that anyone can use to help sort out their own personal values.[4] Examples from this deck of values cards are:

Humility: To be humble and not think of yourself as better than others
Loyalty: To desire and feel and to offer others a strong sense of support or allegiance
Independence: To act with free will based on your own desires and beliefs.

I spoke to Andreea and her business partner, Laura Swapp, about this idea of personal values and how they intersect with work. Andreea and Laura emphasise that in a rapidly changing world, knowing one's values becomes crucial as a guiding anchor amid constant organisational and economic shifts. Like core organisational values, personal values are described as deeply held principles that can act as intrinsic motivators to guide decisions and choices in all of life, both inside and outside work. Andreea and Laura also emphasise that our personal values can influence both the content and trajectory of our careers as well as how people behave at work.

And it's not easy to work at understanding what we value at a personal level. In some cases, we have been so ingrained by societal pressures, parental pressures and our own beliefs about who we should be that we can lose a grip on who we really are and who we want to be.

As we have discussed throughout this book, there are many examples of organisations making the "wrong" choice and acting in a way that is not congruent with what their values say they are about. But behind these organisations are human beings who have made the decision to choose the unethical or the values-misaligned path. These are people who put their personal values on pause. These are real people who saw things and witnessed things and implicitly or explicitly supported behaviours that were probably in contrast to their own values, because they felt cornered or compartmentalised and/or not courageous enough to do what was right.

In other words, these people had unintegrated values. These can weigh a person down and over time make them feel miserable, even leading to burnout. It's analogous to what happens when values at the organisational level led to cultural betrayal. Unintegrated values are about self-betrayal.

So what does alignment between personal values and organisational values look like? Does there have to be perfect alignment between the two? That's probably unrealistic. And your own values can change and shift over time, depending on what your life stage is, with one of your values becoming more predominant than another as life changes. Instead, think about it as a Venn diagram: is there a decent overlap between what you value and what the organisation values? Are there a few of your own values that are non-negotiable and so important to who you are that they would be a deal breaker? If so, are these most important values part of the overlap in our Venn diagram? As Laura and Andreea put it: "Can I find my connection to the organisation's values in that middle space of the Venn diagram?"

Laura Swapp worked briefly for a company that was a very traditional company. She is not a traditionalist. What it took for her to show up every day was a lot more draining because of the work itself and the focus on historical norms and legacy. "I'm much more curious about what's coming next. How do you break things? For me, I don't value legacy in that kind of way. So that was difficult."

In this example, the company was honest about its focus on tradition. What's difficult is that many organisations are not upfront about what is really valued in their organisation, that there isn't always a great alignment between their values on their website and what is valued in the day to day. This can make the comparison a difficult task. A person must dig deeper than what the organisation purports to stand for.

This whole idea presumes a lot. A big presumption is that a person feels as if they have a choice in where they work, in what kind of work they do. There are often so many pressures that people feel when it comes to the jobs they have and where they work that it might not feel like a choice. But if you do feel that you have some choices, it is important to do the work to understand your own personal values first before seeking to find the work culture that is right for you.

At an organisational level, when you're doing culture work, find opportunities for employees to think about their own personal values relative to the organisation's. Encourage them to self-reflect and find where the values overlap. The more that people see themselves in the organisation's culture, the better.

Human connection

Everyone has an innate need to connect with other human beings. And culture, because it is about a shared mindset that happens at the group (not individual) level, is, by definition, about connection. It's about how people are together and what they stand for when they are together. However, it's clear there's a real deficit in how connected people feel; loneliness in life and at work is a sad reality.

A study conducted by Ernst & Young found that more than 80% of employee respondents around the world have felt or feel lonely at work. And almost half (49%) feel lonelier today than they did before the covid pandemic.[5] Besides the obvious sadness of loneliness, there is an impact to the business when employees feel lonely at work. Researchers at California State University and the University of Pennsylvania found that loneliness is related to lower employee commitment and lower performance.[6]

An intentional culture helps people feel like they are part of an integral part of a community. This sense of community transcends job titles and departments, encouraging open communication, collaboration and mutual support. It reinforces a collective purpose, instilling pride and commitment in employees; they start to see themselves as contributors to something bigger. When employees feel connected to their peers and the broader organisation, they are more likely to be engaged and remain committed, contributing to the overall success and sustainability.

When doing culture work, create a sense of belonging with the culture you are working to create. Help people feel a connection to each other. Emphasise unification and working together to achieve the organisation's purpose. Help everyone to see that they matter to the organisation and to each other.

Purpose

Many of us have experience of having work with purpose. Purpose is what allows work to be meaningful and can be understood as "a sense of directedness and intentionality in life".[7] It's why we get up every morning. What feels like purpose can vary greatly from person to person. A sense of purpose can be big or small, long term or short term, local or global. The important thing is that that sense of purpose matters at an individual level.

Purpose is why you do what you do, and values are how you go about achieving your purpose. This is true for both organisations and individuals.

Purpose is an important part of the hearts and minds of culture. The meaning and significance that purpose can help to create can result in a deep emotional connection for people: for their own lives and their personal sense of purpose; for the connection with their colleagues and for their connection to the organisation overall. The terms "meaning" and "purpose" are often used interchangeably, but meaning comes from purpose. Meaningfulness arises from work that gives people a sense of purpose.[8]

I vividly remember one all-hands meeting where our marketing department shared a new video they had created to showcase one of our customers. We were providing enterprise software and were hearing real stories from the people who worked for that customer. They were telling stories about how our software helped them and even helped them change their lives. It was very powerful. It showed that we were making a difference to real human beings. What we worked hard at every day mattered.

There are multiple ways to attain a sense of purpose through our work. The most obvious is through the organisation's mission and purpose. For example, a biotech company that is working to cure Alzheimer's, a human services agency helping with homelessness or a software company supporting mental health. You can also feel a sense of purpose from the way your work is designed or carried out – like a sense of completion or fulfillment when your customers are satisfied or a project comes to an end or when you receive positive feedback from a long-term customer. And of course, you can feel a sense of purpose in how you treat other employees and customers when you do your work. Living your values can be fulfilling and meaningful in and of itself.

People can also feel a sense of purpose when they have

transformational leaders who motivate and help them to see their connection to the organisation's larger vision. And some even have more of a sense of "calling" in their work that transcends the particular company they may be working for at the time.

As we learn more about this sense of purpose there are some important things to understand about it.

First, purpose can come from many other places besides work. Many have a sense of purpose through family or friends or hobbies. But when people find a sense of purpose through work, it's more likely they will be engaged. For example, one study explored how meaningfulness, psychological safety and psychological resource impacted employees' engagement in their work. Results revealed that although all three psychological conditions exhibited a statistically significant positive relationship with employee engagement, meaningfulness was by far the strongest.[9]

Second, purpose is almost always about other human beings; rarely is it about just making money or winning. Though many people think their primary why of working is about these extrinsic (external) motivators, their impact on people continues to be how purpose is manifested. Digging into why we want money or want to win almost always uncovers a human impact somewhere down deep, with underlying motivations rooted in human values, needs and emotions.

Money is often associated with providing a sense of security and comfort. People seek financial stability to ensure their well-being and that of their loved ones – which of course can be connected to purpose. The desire to win or achieve success can also be driven by the need for recognition, self-worth and accomplishment – as a yardstick or proof of worthiness.

Money and success can grant individuals power and

influence, allowing them to make a positive impact on the world or their community, which can be another connection to their purpose. This relates to the human desire for self-actualisation (ie, the realisation of a person's full potential) and the aspiration to make a meaningful difference. For some, accumulating wealth or achieving success goes beyond personal gain. It's about leaving a legacy, making a positive impact on future generations and contributing to the greater good. This relates to the human desire for transcendence and leaving a mark on the world, which is obviously a connection to purpose.

Third, purpose can sometimes be used as a mask for treating people poorly. Some organisations are guilty of preying on employees' deep sense of purpose (eg, for the communities they serve) while not treating those employees with the most basic sense of respect and dignity. If purpose becomes a burden, over time it won't be enough for people to thrive. Purpose needs to go hand in hand with valuing people as human beings.

Fourth, once you are clear about your own purpose, it can be difficult to work in situations that don't align with it. Once you are aware of it, long hours and hard work can feel quite empty without a sense of purpose being fulfilled.

Finally, purpose is related to your well-being. In fact, meaning and purpose in life is a fundamental human desire.[10] The presence of meaning in life promotes psychological health and well-being.[11] One study found that individuals with a strong sense of purpose were better able to cope with stress and adversity, resulting in lower levels of burnout and emotional exhaustion.[12] Purposeful work can be a buffer against the negative impacts of job-related stress, helping people to maintain their well-being and psychological health.[13] And people who feel a sense of purpose tend to be more proactive and persistent in achieving their goals, which can lead to better problem-solving and innovation.[14]

Organisational purpose

Purpose is not only good for people; it's also good for business. A joint research study between Ernst & Young and Harvard Business School found that 58% of companies with a clearly articulated and understood purpose experienced higher growth than companies that did not prioritise it.[15] People are more likely to be drawn to and stay with companies that offer a sense of purpose and a clear connection between their work and the broader impact it has on society.[16] Purpose-driven organisations are also better positioned to build strong relationships with customers and stakeholders because their commitment to a greater cause inspires customer loyalty and support.[17]

I had the opportunity to talk to Barry Schwartz, a social psychologist and author of *Why We Work*, which explores the idea that a paycheque isn't the only reason why we work.

According to Barry, the work itself can be fulfilling and meaningful only if certain conditions are met. The first condition is autonomy. People must have the power and responsibility to make decisions in their day-to-day work (the power sharing explored in Chapter 7). The second is that the organisation must invest in its people's skill development and learning. And third, there must be a mission that people understand and buy into and that they experience authentically across every management level and in what they do every day.

As Barry put it: "You can find a way to make any job feel like it has purpose if you feel heard and appreciated at the place where you're doing the work." He gives an example from the point of view of a sales assistant in a shopping centre. If you think your job is to "sell as much shit as you can", then you're punching a clock. If you think instead that everyone who comes into your store has a problem and your job is to help them solve their problem, doing your job well will improve the lives of 50 or 100 people every day. "That's pretty good to leave work every day feeling that you've made a hundred people's lives better."

Organisations should help people see the importance of their work and how their work lines up to what the purpose of the organisation is. It seems simple and obvious, but most organisations don't take the time to make those connections. I call it "line of sight": connecting the dots between day-to-day work and the mission of the organisation as a whole.

For Barry: "We don't all have to be in the cancer-curing business to find purpose and meaning in what we do, but you have to live up to it as an organisation. If you're not going to praise and promote people who solve problems, and instead you're going to praise and promote people who make sales, then it's very hard to convince yourself that there's any purpose to what you're doing aside from the paycheque you get every two weeks."

KPMG, one of the big four accounting firms, has strategically and intentionally focused on purpose.[18] This has meant crafting a purpose statement and using various methods, including storytelling and visual displays, to help employees connect emotionally to their roles and view their work in a more impactful light. The firm also encourages its employees to share stories of their meaningful contributions, which further strengthens their sense of purpose and belonging.

KPMG also found that those employees whose leaders actively discussed higher purpose exhibited higher engagement levels, underlining the significance of leadership involvement in promoting a sense of purpose. Despite encountering challenges like information overload and leadership scepticism, the firm realised that connecting employees to a meaningful purpose improves performance as well as enhancing engagement. The firm's employee pride measures improved, and it was recognised as a top-ranking company to work for.

The implication for culture work is to connect the culture you are trying to create to the purpose of the organisation. The more that people understand the purpose and emotionally connect and personally relate to it, the more effective the culture work will be.

At the heart of any thriving organisation lies its people; they are the driving force behind its success. Acknowledging the intrinsic value of human beings within the organisational framework is not just essential, it is pivotal to the organisation's purpose. In recognising the significance of human beings, organisations can create a culture that is inherently human-centred. Such a culture transcends mere workplace interactions; it delves deep into the emotions and intellect of employees, creating a profound sense of belonging and purpose.

By placing emphasis on the hearts and minds of their people, organisations can tap into the vast reserves of creativity, innovation and commitment that reside within their workforce.

Remember

1. When doing culture work, it's important to include a focus on human-centred values. The Culture Care Stairs offer some options for ways to weave a focus on human beings into the "aspire to" culture.

2. Focusing on both the hearts and minds of employees is key to culture work. One of the first places to start focusing on

"hearts" is to acknowledge and embrace the important role that emotions play at work.

3. Getting clear about personal values helps towards an understanding of what kind of company culture might be the most suitable.

4. Culture is by definition social. Focus on "hearts" by creating more social connection between employees when conducting culture work.

5. Purpose is the "why" and culture is the "how". Having a strong "why" that employees can emotionally relate to is key to doing great culture work.

Epilogue: Aspirations for better cultures

In this book, I hope I have demonstrated to you that the very nature of organisational culture is what makes it so interesting and so challenging.

Culture is a multifaceted, complex and often misunderstood bundle of attributes that help form a shared mindset of how things are done within an organisation. It is critical for everyone to understand and to be intentional about their cultures because culture guides everyone's behaviour. Being intentional about culture allows organisations to create more clarity, connection and inspiration. Not only does culture matter in helping organisations get better results, but it also affects human beings every day, sometimes creating that connection and inspiration; at other times being so negative that it harms careers, physical health and well-being.

The experience of culture is where many organisations fall short: culture only matters if and how it is experienced. Using the Intentional Culture Circle is a way to operationalise your aspirational culture and to bring it to life in an authentic way. Being intentional also requires a hearts and minds approach – using data and logic, but also connecting with people through emotion, personal values, connection and purpose.

To understand culture, you must also understand power. Power and culture go hand in hand. Leaders, founders, managers and boards need to understand the role that their power plays in influencing the behaviour of employees and should take proactive and intentional steps to use their power to create positive, aligned cultures.

Throughout this book I have referred to "aspire to" culture. I believe that aspiring for a better version of what our day-to-day work can be is a way to embed hope and optimism in our lives. That's what this book is about: when we can paint a picture of what we can be, we are able to start to see it becoming a reality.

Everyone can and should understand culture; it doesn't need to be something that only the C-suite is privy to. We must question it, help form it and work towards it together. As we all seek a deeper connection and more inspiration in our work, there is true power in valuing human beings and being intentional about culture.

Acknowledgements

I'm so grateful to my friends and family for their support while I was working on this book. I'd like to thank my husband, Keith, for his unwavering belief in me and for his ability to entertain himself while I was writing; and my son, Griffin, who read early drafts of my book and gave me some honest feedback that I should write the book like I talk with him about my work. I'm also grateful to my daughter, Skylar, my mom, Marilyn, and dad, Paul, for having no doubts in my abilities, even when I had many.

My wonderful friends Lesley Allan and Sandi Bruha also deserve a big thank you. They both checked in on me, encouraged me and reminded me how cool this opportunity is. I'd also like to thank Becki Hamill and Sophie Mitkevitch for helping me find real examples of how culture impacts human beings.

Special acknowledgment goes to Clare Grist Taylor, the editor of this book. Her feedback and suggestions not only enhanced the content but also left me in awe of her skill.

Finally, I'd like to thank all the people who shared their stories with me in this book and the endless people who have reminded me how important this topic is.

Notes

Chapter 1: Defining culture

1. D. Sull, C. Sull and B. Zweig, "Toxic culture is driving the great resignation", *MIT Sloan Management Review* (January 11th 2022).
2. E.H. Schein, *The Corporate Culture Survival Guide* (San Francisco, CA: Jossey-Bass, 2009).
3. B. Groysberg et al., "The leader's guide to corporate culture", *Harvard Business Review* (January–February 2018).
4. B. Schneider, D.B. Smith and H.W. Goldstein, "Attraction–selection–attrition: toward a person–environment psychology of organizations" in W.B. Walsh, K.H. Craik and R.H. Price (eds), *Person–Environment Psychology: New Directions and Perspectives* (Lawrence Erlbaum Associates, 2000), pp. 61–85.
5. "North American airline passenger satisfaction declines", J.D. Power, press release (May 11th 2022).
6. G. Johnson, R. Whittington and K. Scholes, *Fundamentals of Strategy* (Harlow, Essex: Pearson Education, 2012).
7. K. Weber and M.T. Dacin, "The cultural construction of organizational life: introduction to the special issue", *Organization Science*, 22(2) (2011), pp. 287–98.
8. For example: C.A. Hartnell et al., "Organizational culture and organizational effectiveness: a meta-analytic investigation of the competing values framework's theoretical suppositions", *Journal of Applied Psychology*, 96(4) (2011), pp. 677–94.

Chapter 2: Culture as an experience

1. C. Ostroff, A.J. Kinicki and R.S. Muhammad, *Organizational Culture and Climate*, Volume 12. *Industrial and Organizational Psychology IV. The Work Environment* (2012). doi.org/10.1002/9781118133880. hop212024

2. A. Swidler, "Culture in action: symbols and strategies", *American Sociological Review*, 51(2) (1986), pp. 273–86.
3. A. Bick, A. Blandin and K. Mertens, "Work from home after the COVID-19 outbreak", Working Paper, Federal Reserve Bank of Dallas (2020).
4. A. Ozimek, "Future workforce report 2021: how remote work is changing businesses forever", Upwork.com (2021).
5. Owl Labs, "State of remote work report (2021)", owllabs.com (2021).
6. Ergotron, "The evolving office: empower employees to work vibrantly in 2022", ebook, Ergotron.com (2021). www2.ergotron.com/EEWVWP2022
7. D. Banerjee and M. Rai, "Social isolation in Covid-19: the impact of loneliness", *International Journal of Social Psychiatry*, 66(6) (2020), pp.525–7.
8. V. Di Martino and L. Wirth, "Telework: a new way of working and living", *International Labour Review*, 129(5) (1990), pp. 529–54.
9. J. Teevan et al. (eds). "Microsoft new future of work report 2022", Microsoft Research Tech Report MSR-TR-2022-3 (2022).
10. T. O'Brien, Interview about how technology can help form culture (December 1st 2022).

Chapter 3: Why culture matters
1. From J.P. Kotter and J.L. Heskett, *Corporate Culture and Performance* (New York: Free Press, 1992). Copyright © 1992 by Kotter Associates Inc. and James L. Heskett. Reprinted with the permission of The Free Press, an imprint of Simon & Schuster. All rights reserved.
2. D. Sull and C. Sull, "Culture 500: introducing the 2020 culture champions", *MIT Sloan Management Review* (October 13th 2020).
3. J.R. Graham et al., "Corporate culture: evidence from the field", *Journal of Financial Economics*, 146(2) (2022), pp. 552–93.
4. D.G. White, *Disrupting Corporate Culture: How cognitive science alters accepted beliefs about culture and culture change and its impact on leaders and change agents* (New York: Routledge, 2021).
5. D. Sull, C. Sull and B. Zweig, "Toxic culture is driving the great resignation", *MIT Sloan Management Review* (January 11th 2022).
6. C.A. Montgomery and A.V. Whillans, "France Télécom (B): a wave of staff suicides", Harvard Business School Supplement 721-421 (December 2020).

7. D. Sull et al., "Why every leader needs to worry about toxic culture", *MIT Sloan Management Review* (March 16th 2022).
8. D. Sull and C. Sull, "How to fix a toxic culture", *MIT Sloan Management Review* (September 28th 2022).
9. Reprinted from D.L. Paulhus and K.M. Williams, "The dark triad of personality: narcissism, Machiavellianism and psychopathy", *Journal of Research in Personality*, 36(6) (2002), pp. 556–63. Copyright © 2002, with permission from Elsevier. Reprinted from *The Lancet*.
10. S. Taylor, "The danger of dark triad leaders", *Psychology Today* (March 5th 2022).
11. V. Ratanjee, "How to build trust in the workplace", Gallup.com (June 14th 2022).
12. L. Myers, "What is an ounce of integrity worth in a manager?", *Cornell Chronicle* (November 2nd 2000).
13. R.M. Galford and A.S. Drapeau, "The enemies of trust", *Harvard Business Review* (February 2003).

Chapter 4: Are you ready to change?

1. R. Boohene and A.A. Williams, "Resistance to organisational change: a case study of Oti Yeboah Complex Limited", *International Business and Management*, 4(1) (2012), pp. 135–45.
2. S.B. Sarason, *Revisiting "The Culture of the School and the Problem of Change"* (New York: Teachers College Press, 1996).
3. "The 8 steps for leading change", kotterinc.com
4. Kübler-Ross Change Curve®, ekrfoundation.org
5. The Prosci ADKAR® Model, prosci.com
6. J. Clear, *Atomic Habits: Tiny Changes, Remarkable Results: An easy & proven way to build good habits & break bad ones* (New York: Avery, Penguin Random House, 2018).

Chapter 5: Intention: Setting the stage for culture evolution

1. N. Bek, "'Tableau has been killed by Salesforce': past and current Tableau employees gather at 'Irish wake'", Geekwire.com (February 13th 2023).

Chapter 6: Bringing culture to life

1. M. Beer, "To change your company culture, don't start by trying to change the culture", Harvard Business School Working Knowledge (December 14th 2021).
2. J. Zhou and J.M. George, "When job dissatisfaction leads to creativity: encouraging the expression of voice", *Academy of Management Journal*, 44(4) (2001), pp. 682–96.
3. K.S. Cameron and R.E. Quinn, *Diagnosing and Changing Organizational Culture: Based on the competing values framework* (San Francisco, CA: Jossey-Bass, 2006).
4. M.K. Linnenluecke and A. Griffiths, "Corporate sustainability and organizational culture", *Journal of World Business*, 45(4) (2010), pp. 357–66.
5. T.G. Cummings and C.G. Worley, *Organization Development and Change* (Cengage Learning, 2014).
6. L. Goler et al., "Why people really quit their jobs", *Harvard Business Review* (January 11th 2018).
7. Glassdoor Mission and Culture Survey 2019, "New survey: company mission & culture matter more than salary", Glassdoor.co.uk (July 11th 2019).
8. Qualtrics, "Employees who feel aligned with company values are more likely to stay", qualtrics.com (April 25th 2022).
9. B. Morgan, "The five lessons from Trader Joe's unbeatable customer experience", Forbes (October 24th 2019).

Chapter 7: Culture and power

1. C. Rhodes, "Democratic business ethics: Volkswagen's emissions scandal and the disruption of corporate sovereignty", *Organization Studies*, 37 (10) (2016), pp. 1501–18.
2. J.R.P. French and B.H. Raven, "The bases of social power" in D.E. Cartwright (ed.), *Studies in Social Power* (Ann Arbor, MI: Institute for Social Research, 1959), pp. 150–67.
3. R. Bates, "Culture and leadership in educational administration: a historical study of what was and what might have been", *Journal of Education Administration and History*, 38(2) (2006), pp. 155–68.
4. This funny take on how all the biggest tech companies are organised comes from cartoonist Manu Cornet, via Foursquare product chief

Alex Rainert. See "The org charts of all the major tech companies (humor)", Businessinsider.com (June 29th 2011).

5. N. Reiff, "Decentralized autonomous organization (DAO): definition, purpose, and example", Investopedia.com (September 30th 2023).
6. D.M. Rousseau, "Psychological and implied contracts in organisations", *Employee Responsibilities and Rights Journal*, 2 (1989), pp. 121–39.
7. G. Hofstede, G.J. Hofstede and M. Minkov, *Cultures and Organizations: Software of the Mind*, 3rd edn (McGraw-Hill, 2010).
8. E. Nocos, "Japanese corporate culture", Scalingyourcompany.com (July 30th 2023).
9. "Work life balance", Passport to Trade 2.0. businessculture.org/ northern-europe/sweden/work-life-balance/
10. H. Simon, "Lessons from Germany's midsize giants", *Harvard Business Review* (March–April 1992).
11. "Culture as a corporate asset", National Association of Corporate Directors report (NACD, 2017).
12. F. Laloux, *Reinventing Organizations: A Guide to Creating Organizations Inspired by the Next Stage of Human Consciousness* (Nelson Parker, 2014).
13. "I, Tomato: Morning Star's radical approach to management", Enlivening Edge, Enliveningedge.org (January 15th 2016).
14. M.A. Azevedo, "Untapped opportunity: minority founders still being overlooked", Crunchbase News, crunchbase.com (February 27th 2019).
15. "The state of European tech 2020". 2019.stateofeuropeantech.com/ chapter/diversity-inclusion/
16. "Founder demographics and statistics in the US", Zippia, zippia.com
17. L. Stefano, "Only 15% of tech startup founders are female", Startup Genome, Startupgenome.com (March 27th 2023).
18. K. Rosman and K. Belson, "Promised a new culture, woman say the N.F.L. instead pushed them aside", *New York Times* (February 8th 2022).
19. L.H. Nishii, D.P. Lepak and B. Schneider, "Employee attributions of the 'why' of HR practices: their effects on employee attitudes and behaviors, and customer satisfaction", *Personnel Psychology*, 61(3) (2008), pp. 503–45.

20. S.G. Cohen and D.E. Bailey, "What makes teams work: group effectiveness research from the shop floor to the executive suite", *Journal of Management*, 23(3) (1997), pp. 239–90.
21. S. Bertels, J. Howard-Grenville and S. Pek, "Cultural molding, shielding, and shoring at Oilco: the role of culture in the integration of routines", *Organization Science*, 27(3) (2016), pp. 573–93.
22. W. Zhang et al., "Understanding how organizational culture affects innovation performance: a management context perspective", *Sustainability*, 15(8) (2023), p. 6644.
23. S. Pichai, "Our commitments to racial equity", Google blog (June 17th 2020).
24. Google, "2022 Diversity Annual Report". about.google/belonging/ diversity-annual-report/2022/

Chapter 8: Rethinking cultural assumptions

1. D. Sull, C. Sull and B. Zweig, "Toxic culture is driving the great resignation", *MIT Sloan Management Review* (January 11th 2022).
2. L.A. Rivera, "Hiring as cultural matching: the case of elite professional service firms", *American Sociological Review* 77(6) (2012), pp. 999–1022.
3. D.G. White, *Disrupting Corporate Culture: How cognitive science alters accepted beliefs about culture and culture change and its impact on leaders and change agents* (New York: Routledge, 2021).

Chapter 9: Valuing humans

1. A.R. Hochschild, *The Managed Heart: Commercialization of Human Feeling* (University of California Press, 1983).
2. S. Hays, "American Express taps into the power of emotional intelligence", Workforce.com (July 1st 1999).
3. N.M. Ashkanasy and A.D. Dorris, "Emotions in the workplace", *Annual Review of Organizational Psychology and Organizational Behavior*, 4(1) (2017), pp. 67–90.
4. A. Niculescu and L. Congdon, *The Live Your Values Deck: Sort Out, Honor and Practice What Matters Most to You* (Chronicle Books, 2022).
5. EY Global, "The Asia-Pacific Belonging Barometer 2022 highlights a growing talent gap between employees' needs and organizations' cultures", ey.com (December 7th 2022).

6. H. Ozcelik and S.G. Barsade, "No employee an island: workplace loneliness and job performance", *Academy of Management Journal*, 61(6) (2018), pp. 2343–66.

7. B.D. Rosso, K.H. Dekas and A. Wrzesniewski, "On the meaning of work: a theoretical integration and review", *Research in Organizational Behavior*, 30(5) (2010), pp. 91–127.

8. B.J. Dik, Z.S. Byrne and M.F. Steger (eds), *Purpose and Meaning in the Workplace* (Washington, DC: American Psychological Association, 2013).

9. D.R. May, R.L. Gilson and L.M. Harter, "The psychological conditions of meaningfulness, safety and availability and the engagement of the human spirit at work", *Journal of Occupational and Organizational Psychology*, 77(1) (2004), pp. 11–37.

10. Ozcelik and Barsade, "No employee an island"; Rosso et al., "On the meaning of work".

11. M.F. Steger et al., "The meaning in life questionnaire: assessing the presence of and search for meaning in life", *Journal of Counseling Psychology*, 53(1) (2006), pp. 80–93.

12. R.F. Baumeister et al., "Some key differences between a happy life and a meaningful life", *Journal of Positive Psychology*, 8(6) (2013), pp. 505–16.

13. M.G. Pratt and B.E. Ashforth, "Fostering meaningfulness in working and at work", in K.S. Cameron, J.E. Dutton and R.E. Quinn (eds), *Positive Organizational Scholarship: Foundations of a New Discipline* (Oakland, CA: Berrett-Koehler, 2003), pp. 309–27.

14. A.M. Grant and S.K. Parker, "Redesigning work design theories: the rise of relational and proactive perspectives", *Academy of Management Annals*, 3(1) (2009), pp. 317–75.

15. Pratt and Ashforth, "Fostering meaningfulness".

16. Ozcelik and Barsade, "No employee an island".

17. V. Keller, "The business case for purpose", Harvard Business Review Analytical Services Report (2015).

18. B.N. Pfau, "How an accounting firm convinced its employees they could change the world", *Harvard Business Review* (October 6th 2015).

Index

Unless otherwise specified, all headings relate to the concept of culture at work.
Page references for diagrams appear in *italics*.

drumbeats 85, 111, 130

E
education 84–5, 98–101
emails 22, 93, 99
embedded culture 129–30
emotion
  at work 190–93
  connecting with people 81
  emotional labour 191
  emotional resonance 192
  Kübler-Ross Change Curve 76–8
  reaction to the culture and
    workplace 24, 42, 98
  wellbeing 37
employee resource groups (ERGs)
  161
employees
  actual experience of 9
  Alan Mulally at Ford 11–12, 13
  aspire to culture and 20
  attrition 13, 38, 58, 74
  autonomy, need for 201
  benefits 116
  better outcomes for 33
  compensation 119–20
  cultural voids and 36
  culture and 15, 22–3, 28, 43
  disconnects 22–3, 74–5
  engagement from 42–3
  Ernst & Young 12–13
  experiencing the culture 38
  handbooks 117
  hiring of 115
  job seekers 111
  joining a new firm 25–6, 44
  leadership interaction 14
  learning the culture 28

  managers and 46
  networks 117
  power and 140–41, 150–54
  promotion 106
  recognition 122–3
  reimbursements 118
  responses of 27
  rewards systems 119–24
  second jobs 145
  shared mindsets 15–16
  Southwest Airlines 24–5
  termination 117
  working from home and 44
  working together 13–14
engagement 41–3
  emotions and 191
  factors 199
  lack of 74
  trust and 63
Enron 123
Ernst & Young (EY) 12–13, 196, 201
experiences 112–14
  articulated v experienced 36–8
  "aspire to" culture and 129
  authentic 130
  big and small 107
  culture and 20
  culture triangles *140*
  defining 85
  employees never so clear about
    13
  importance of 33
  Intentional Culture Circle *84,
    89, 107*
  NFL 156
  Our Way (Clotia Robinson) 158
  senior leaders 155
  trust and 66

W
well-being 37, 200
Whillans, Ashley 59
White, David 180
Whittington, Richard 26, 28
Why We Work (Barry Schwartz) 200
Williams, Asamoah 71
Williams, Kevin 134

whole person 188
working from home *see* remote working
work–life balance 141
workplace 44–5, 47, 52
Woven Planet 124–6

Z
Zoom 47, 49, 54

About the author

Laura Hamill is an organisational psychologist and business leader who focuses on the intersection of science and HR with a specific emphasis on employee well-being, engagement and organisational culture.

Laura is the owner of Paris Phoenix Group, a consulting firm that specialises in driving impactful research and outcomes. In her consulting business, Laura has worked with numerous organisations to assess and transform their cultures. She is a co-founder of Limeade, an employee experience software company, where she held the dual roles of Chief People Officer and Chief Science Officer. Before Limeade, Laura worked at Microsoft as Director of People Research.

She is a sought-after thought leader and speaker. She has been the keynote speaker at major tech and HR conferences, and featured in Fast Company, Forbes, HR Executive Inc., NPR, SELF, US News & World Report and other top HR publications. Laura is also a host on the Happy at Work podcast.

Laura earned her PhD and MS in industrial and organisational psychology from Old Dominion University and a BA in psychology from the University of North Carolina, Chapel Hill. She lives near Seattle, Washington, with her husband, two children and golden retriever.

Learn more about Laura and her work at
www.parisphoenixgroup.com